What O

"Your leadership journey begins with you. Real leaders are rare indeed. If you want to have more impact with the people you serve best, it starts with a single step and then another and another. In your hands you hold a path and a plan for becoming an influential leader. What are you waiting for?"

—**Mark LeBlanc, speaker, and author of *Never be the Same* and *Build Your Consulting Practice*.**

"Nothing significant ever happens alone—and that includes your development. Jim has provided a simple, practical guide filled with goodness! It will help you develop your own team of mentors to help you grow in all areas of your life."

—**Paul Batz, inspiring speaker, best-selling author, executive coach, and founder and CEO of Good Leadership Enterprises and host of The Good Leadership Breakfast.**

"Leaders don't get to the top on their own. You should have a team of mentors—your own personal board. Your ability to successfully navigate life will be greatly enhanced with the wisdom and experience from others who are willing to walk the journey with you. Live out the model of mentorship and then pay it forward to the next generation. Follow the path in *Peak Perspective* and let it guide you to customizing your own personal board and lead others in a meaningful way."

—**Robert Lewis, pastor, speaker, and author of *Men's Fraternity, Raising a Modern Day Knight,* and *The Church of Irresistible Influence*.**

"*Peak Perspective* is an insightful read that demonstrates how value-based relationships are critical to your personal and professional growth. It underscores that great leaders truly need wingmen—trusted partners in their life they can go to for help, advice, and honest feedback. Make it part of your flight plan for success."

—Lt. Col. Rob "Waldo" Waldman, author of the New York Times and Wall Street Journal bestseller, *Never Fly Solo*.

"Isolation is fatal! Don't go it alone. At a time when our thirst for mentors has never been greater, this book offers an oasis of guidance on how to grow and give on purpose."

—Richard J. Leider, international bestselling author of *The Power of Purpose*, *Repacking Your Bags*, and *Life Reimagined*.

"Zugschwert hits the mark! People need one another to succeed and interdependence, not independence, is an essential part of becoming a trusted leader! His take on having a personal board is powerful and relevant. I resonate with *Peak Perspective* because this idea has been crucial to the success I have enjoyed both professionally and personally."

—David Horsager, international speaker and author of *The Trust Edge* and *The Daily Edge*.

"The best leaders in the world have two qualities—they are well-grounded and well-surrounded. Jim Zugschwert hits a homerun by taking a known concept, a Board of Directors, and applying it in an uncharted way. Our world desperately needs a new generation of "well-surrounded" leaders—leaders who understand that *Peak Perspective* leads to peak performance. This is a must-read for everyone on your team."

—**Scott Hagan, President of North Central University, international speaker, and author of** *The Language of Influence.*

"Everyone should have a team on their side. *Peak Perspective* is the guide to building your own team of mentors. Jim provides a step-by-step process to gaining new ground in your quest for developing as a leader by surrounding yourself with those who have your best interests in mind."

—**Kit Welchlin, keynote speaker, seminar leader, and author of** *The Communication Kit—Volumes 1 and 2.*

"If you are tired from spending years trying to figure out your way on the path of life with no one to turn to for guidance, this book is for you. Jim leads you on a journey to grow personally and professionally by providing a road map that you can customize for your own life."

—**Shaun Irwin, author of** *Convertible Referrals* **and owner of Anderson Agency, Minneapolis, Minnesota.**

PEAK PERSPECTIVE

Make a difference on your journey!
Go. Climb. Grow. Lead. Give

PEAK PERSPECTIVE

Develop Your Personal
Board of Directors
And Become the Leader
You Were Meant to Be

JIM ZUGSCHWERT

Printed in the United States of America

Published by Author Academy Elite
P.O. Box 43, Powell, OH 43035

www.AuthorAcademyElite.com

Paperback ISBN: 978-1-64085-244-0
Hardcover ISBN: 978-1-64085-245-7

Library of Congress Control Number: 2018935501

Author Academy Elite, Powell, OH

Scripture quotations are taken from the Holy Bible, New Living Translation, copyright © 1996. Used by permission of Tyndale House Publishers, Inc., Wheaton, Illinois 60189. All rights reserved.

The Internet addresses in this book are accurate at the time of publication. They are provided as a resource. Jim Zugschwert or the publisher do not endorse them or vouch for their content or permanence.

To my late father, Eugene

and to my mother Marge Zugschwert,

who raised me with a foundation

of family, friends, and faith.

Thanks for teaching me to love life, give to others,

and for sharing the joy of laughter.

—

CONTENTS

PART THREE: HIGHER VIEW — LEAD ON

"*You are not here merely to make a living. You are here in order to enable the world to live more amply, with greater vision, with a finer spirit of hope and achievement. You are here to enrich the world, and you impoverish yourself if you forget the errand.*"

--Woodrow Wilson--

INTRODUCTION

JUST A NORMAL THURSDAY

Defining Moments. We all have them, even when they aren't immediately recognizable. In a transition, tragedy, or opportunity in our lives, we are so often caught up in the moment at hand we don't always understand what's really happening.

What started out as simply another normal Thursday turned into a defining moment for me. On June 14, 2012, I was called into a meeting with my boss and the CEO of the company where I had been working for nearly nine years. We walked down the hall to the board room and the three of us sat at the end of the large table with the CEO at the head and my boss across from me. My boss opened the discussion with a review of the current state of the economy. He went on to address the importance of protecting the financial stability of the company and the members, etc.

It was barely two minutes into the meeting when I thought to myself, "Oh my, this is about me!" After a few more points were brought up regarding the challenges that needed to be addressed, my boss handed the conversation over to the CEO. As he struggled to even look at me the CEO said, "This is the toughest part of my job. There is no easy way to say this so I'm just going to say it...."

Losing a job is never easy.

What was truly amazing about that day was not what had happened in that meeting. It's what I had done four years earlier that made all the difference!

▲

Mentorship – A New Definition

Four years earlier I had been invited to join a group of businessmen meeting weekly for a study called, *The Great Adventure*—the third year of *Men's Fraternity*, a three-year curriculum by Robert Lewis. This series taught principles of biblical manhood to guide us to discover and live our own great adventure for the rest of our lives and beyond.

It was in this setting that I had a revelation.

In Session 3, Lewis said, "It would be good for you, as one man suggested to me, that you create your own personal board. Two or three guys that are not 'yes' men."[1]

BOOM!

This idea struck me in a profound way. I had never heard of a personal board. What a wonderful picture of having a team of my very own—to seek guidance from and bounce ideas off of—in order to increase my ability to make quality decisions for my personal and professional life.

I wanted people like that in my life! I immediately began to lay out a roadmap for building my *personal Board of Directors*.

My mind swirled with questions: Who? How? Why? When?

I knew the importance of being strategic and not random about who would join my personal board, and I set out to discover the best practices to build a mentor team in this way.

This journey helped me years later to handle my job loss and move ahead with confidence. I want to give this same gift to you. I want you to have a BOOM experience!

Through this process you will learn how to prepare yourself to handle whatever life throws at you. You don't have to go it alone.

▲

Prepare Your Field

In 2007, Alex and Stephen Kendrick came out with their second movie, *Facing the Giants.* This inspirational movie about living your life for a purpose higher than yourself helped solidify the idea in my mind of preparing and building a team even before opposition arrived.

In the movie, Coach Grant Taylor is approached by a man, Mr. Bridges, who shared with him a story to ponder in the face of the impending opposition before him:

"Grant, I heard a story about two farmers who desperately needed rain, and both of them prayed for rain. But only one of them went out to his field to prepare to receive it. Which one do you think trusted God to send the rain?" Grant replied, "Well, the one who prepared his field for it."

Mr. Bridges asked, "Which one are you? God will send the rain when He's ready. You need to prepare your field to receive it."[2]

Taking action in preparation for your future gives you flexibility and freedom to respond to circumstances with a minimum of despair. Having your own team of mentors will ultimately prepare you to handle any hurdle you face. Preparing your field means that no matter what life brings your way, whether a challenge or an opportunity, you will be able to handle it with confidence, guidance, and support. You won't have to face it by yourself.

What you will discover in this book is a road map, a proven plan, to help your professional and personal development in ways that you could never accomplish on your own. It's time to be intentional about building and engaging your own personal Board of Directors in order to expand your perspective and strengthen your capacity and ability to lead others.

I will show you how to get yourself connected with others who can be impact players in helping you expand your thinking and deepen your perspective in all aspects of your life.

We all think we can do it alone. What we often fail to realize is that we need each other to grow. Floating along by yourself will not get you where you want to go. It's time to take action and engage others who are willing to join you, get to know you, and guide you in your journey.

You may already have people in your life who you confide in when you face a challenge or opportunity. I want to help you be as effective and strategic as possible as you engage with these friends, counselors, and mentors. I want to help you confirm whether or not those you already confide in will qualify to be on your personal board.

Remember, this book is not about them. This book about YOU!

This is about your personal Board of Directors.

This is your path to new heights. You will learn to climb to higher ground and expand your perspective. You will find open doors and willing hands to pull you up and guide you as you learn from the wisdom, insight, and experience of others. Through this process you will grow to a point of wanting to give back and lead others with impact.

This is your personal and professional journey to becoming the leader you were meant to be.

▲

PART ONE

CHALLENGE

ALL ALONE

CHAPTER 1
ON YOUR OWN

*"No individual has any right to come into this world
and go out of it without leaving behind him distinct
and legitimate reasons for having passed through it."*

--George Washington Carver--

As long as I can remember, I've had to share. I grew up as the third oldest of nine kids. With four brothers and four sisters, I was surrounded at every turn. This didn't mean I didn't ever get my way. It simply meant that life always seemed to be a compromise. Consideration had to be given to the common good of the family.

Having had nine kids in twelve years, I believed that my mother and father had already qualified for sainthood. They were two extraordinary people who loved a big family and worked hard to build each of us up under family principles of love and care for each other, while still allowing us to grow as individuals.

In our early years, they took on the challenge of making our birthdays as unique and special to us as they could. We all looked forward to this as the one day each year we could approach—if only just a little—calling our own shots.

It was over rather quickly as no sibling was safe the day after their birthday. The birthday gifts seemed to be up for grabs starting with the sunrise the very next day, especially when it came to clothes. My older brother and I were only a year apart and nearly the same size in our younger years. If I put my shirt or jersey in the laundry and didn't pay attention to it when it came out, it was just as likely to be worn by him as by me.

In some ways, this had caused me to develop an inability to work well and play well with others, simply because I was hungry for my own identity. The dynamics of my big family became a training ground where I learned to do things for myself and by myself. I wanted to break out from the crowd and be known for who *I* was and didn't need or want help from anyone. I could handle it all on my own, thank you very much!

The more possessive I became, the harder it was for me to tackle projects together with someone else. I usually wanted to handle it in my own way and in my own time. Some would consider this isolationist behavior; for me, it was simply my way of not having to share.

Years later in the world of work, I found this pattern to be more of a hindrance than a help when approaching a challenge with only my own perspective and experience to guide me. These were the days long before the internet, when we couldn't turn to online videos or blog posts to gain additional perspective. We had to either consult with a professional or simply wing it and try our best.

Little did I know this idea of not sharing and regularly claiming things to be "mine" would become an issue to address even when I got married. Yours, mine and *ours*? Seriously?

I had a lot of growing up to do.

▲

Worlds Apart

In my career in sales I have had two job-loss experiences that couldn't have been more opposite. The first one happened in 1998 when I was all alone in my thinking with no team of mentors around me. I had a young family and very little savings and we had to depend on others to help us financially. It was an embarrassing and humiliating time. I thought I had all the answers and yet I didn't know what to do. My wife just wanted me to do "something!" Eventually, I found a job and slowly started to move forward.

Two jobs and fourteen years later, I found myself in the board room (as described in the introduction) learning that I was being let go. The difference was that I already had built my own personal Board of Directors. In the days and weeks following that meeting I experienced a tidal wave of value wash over me. Virtually every day for the first two weeks after I lost my job I met with or spoke with one or more of my five board members. It was an amazing time of connection, reflection and planning that filled me with confidence and allowed me to move quickly into another job that was a better opportunity for me and my family. My wife observed that my attitude, motivation, and action plan were worlds apart from my unemployment journey in 1998.

I was also reminded of the impact on those around me, especially in the challenging times from the previous job loss. When challenges come, this is not the time to remain on your own in your thinking. I was so concerned with myself that I missed the fact that my wife and family were also watching me flounder in my own thinking.

It took me years to figure out I was going about this the wrong way. I am grateful to my wife, my parents, and the key men in my life today for their love, patience, and desire to help and encourage me on my journey to climb higher, both personally and professionally. They have helped me recognize the true value in opening myself up to the wisdom, insight, and experience of others as a vital strategy rather than a crutch or a sign of weakness.

Have you found yourself carrying the burden of your childhood as an excuse for your current outcomes in life? Is this just your lot in life? Are you struggling to see a different path? Do you think you'll have to settle for who you are right now? Or, can it be different? Is it possible that you are on the threshold of something amazing?

This is your journey.

You get to decide how you respond to whatever life throws at you.

You are the result of decisions you've made and those you've neglected to make up to this point in your life. Remember that no decision is still a decision—a decision to do nothing! The good news is that you can also decide at any time to change the path for your future by changing your thinking and changing how you respond to life.

▲

It Starts with You

If you have found yourself wondering how to let others into your life, you're not alone. When faced with some of my greatest personal challenges, even recognizing that I needed to change, I didn't know how to go about seeking advice from others.

Who can I share this with?

Who can I trust?

Who really cares?

Who is willing to listen and not jump in and prescribe a solution?

Some of my hesitation in seeking help from others to discuss my issues came from the poor connections I had made in the past. I had connected with people who seemed more interested in telling me what to do. They thought their age, or their experience would allow them to step in and give me the answer to my problems. Believe it or not, this only slowed me down.

I realized that their suggested solutions were really a disguise for opinions wrapped in a lack of information about my circumstances. They thought they knew what my issues were, yet they never asked questions to clarify or better understand my concerns or what my own questions were.

But maybe it was me. Maybe it was the way I went about it.

I found when I asked people what they thought, they usually told me what they thought and then immediately went into what I should do about it. This was a leap that often left me feeling defensive. I quickly shut down and didn't listen to any form of advice. I wanted perspective and counsel, but I didn't know how to go about getting it. This was my plight throughout my thirties and into my forties.

Have you ever felt that no one was listening to you? Did it seem as though people were more interested in dishing out solutions rather than getting more information and trying to connect? This can be a lonely feeling. It can lead to a lack of trust in others and in their motives.

It's time to consider a new way of thinking.

In his book *Thinking for a Change*, John C. Maxwell provides a powerful case and a platform to help you start thinking differently. He says, "The greatest detriment to many people's success tomorrow is their thinking today. If their thinking is limited, so is their potential. But if people can keep growing in their thinking, they will constantly outgrow what they're doing. And their potential will always be off the charts."[1]

Making decisions based on only your own perspective often brings limited results. Sadly, we don't always see the limitations of our outcomes until we reflect on the results, even if it's years later. Being open to trust others takes courage. It also requires being intentional. You get to decide on the timing of your journey. Why not start with today?

Starting today, make a new decision.

Starting today, change your thinking.

Starting today, choose your path.

▲

No One Can Live Your Life for You

It's your life and it's up to you to go where you want to go and dream what you want to dream. No one can live it for you. This may seem to be a simple statement; however, it's more than that—it's really an important truth. If you find yourself wondering what you really want out of life or what your next chapter should be, this is a perfect time to start engaging the counsel of others.

You don't have to know all the answers. Good counsel can lead you to good decisions. Take the case of Lieutenant Colonel Rob "Waldo" Waldman, who overcame his fears and became a decorated fighter pilot, author, speaker, and coach. In his book, *Never Fly Solo*, he addresses the power of having others in your corner—your wingmen—to help you navigate through exciting and challenging times.

Waldman writes, "We all have fears, doubts, and self-limiting beliefs that hold us back from breaking the performance barrier in our work and in our lives. Yet it's the relationships we build and the people whom we trust that give us the courage to take risks and make ourselves better …. It is, above all else, about building trust in yourself and then building trusting relationships with others. These trusted partners, male or female, are your wingmen."[2]

Developing your team of wingmen is a great way to help you realize how important it is to change your thinking from going it alone to building a team.

It took me a while, but I eventually realized I owned all my decisions, both good and bad. The reality of that statement in my own life was sometimes more haunting than I cared to admit. After all, these were my results. I couldn't complain to anyone else about my circumstances because, as a soloist, I owned all my outcomes.

What I was seeking had to come from the inside. I had to change. No one else could do it for me. I had to reshape my thinking instead of doing the same thing over and over again. I had to open myself up to others and start asking questions and sharing what was really on my heart.

I am not a proponent of living with regret. I much prefer to think of my circumstances as part of my story. Taking responsibility for myself and figuring out what I really wanted was a slow journey for me. It was my life, and I had to learn that living it in isolation was not the way to go. Once I embraced the fact that it is my life and no one else can live it for me, I decided to look into the process that champions went through on their journey to the top.

▲

Champions Legacy

I have always enjoyed sports and loved to hear and read about the journey of discipline and hard work that goes into being prepared for competition. I became fascinated with the work behind the scenes that made the difference when it counted—from examining Muhammed Ali's training regimen to the relentless work of Ben Hogan hitting golf balls on the range to perfect his swing. I examined the repetition of the fundamentals of the top baseball players. I enjoyed learning about the differences between the finesse of a shortstop and the need for powerful legs as a key foundation for successful pitchers.

I fell in love with golf when I was around 10 years old. I grew up during the rise of Jack Nicklaus as he battled many greats, including Arnold Palmer, Gary Player, Tom Watson, Lee Trevino, and so many others. I started reading about how Nicklaus' approach was different than virtually all of the other players on the PGA Tour. His 1983 book, *Jack Nicklaus' Playing Lessons*, explained the importance of his mental preparation, especially how he strategically prepared for the four major championships each year.

I loved the strategy and pictures of the fundamentals of golf in this book. What surprised me was how much I enjoyed learning about his mindset.

Here, in his own words, is a glimpse of one the most important perspectives I learned from Nicklaus regarding the visualization of executing a golf shot as he quoted from his book, *Golf My Way*:

"I never hit a shot, even in practice, without having a very sharp, in-focus picture of it in my head. It's like a color movie. First I *see* where I want it to finish, nice and white and sitting up high on the bright green grass. Then the scene quickly changes and I *see* the ball going there: its path, trajectory, and shape, even its behavior on landing. Then there is this sort of fadeout, and the next scene shows me making the kind of swing that will turn the previous image to reality."[3]

Wow! What a powerful reality of a powerful mindset. His attention to every detail was amazing. Nicklaus' discipline was relentless, and his daily attitude displayed his great appreciation for the game of golf. When Bobby Jones, the greatest amateur golfer in history, was asked about the play of a young Jack Nicklaus, he said, "He plays a game with which I am not familiar."[4]

Who are the champions in your own life that you look up to? Where did they come from? What sets them apart? Study their habits. Learn their strategies. Begin to change your thinking and strive to learn from them. It doesn't matter whether they come from your family, business or industry, sports, entertainment, or even a teacher or coach from your own upbringing.

There are many examples in and around your life if you just pay attention to them.

▲

Begin to Think Bigger

It's time to say goodbye to going it alone. If your primary counselors are *Me, Myself, and I,* you're not thinking big enough. Once you realize you need the perspective of others, you'll start to change the way you approach situations.

A common challenge I discovered in myself was my habit of asking the opinion of those who would normally agree with me. My own team of "yes" men made it seem like I was expanding my perspective, but instead, it was still very self-serving.

In order to grow, I had to realize I actually wanted to learn from the wisdom and experience of others even if they thought differently or disagreed with me. I started looking around my life and began asking questions of others, like:

• How did you get started with your company?

- Have you always worked in this industry?
- What led you to specialize in _____?
- Have you always been interested in this field?
- What do you like to do in your spare time?

One of my favorite combinations of questions was built around the idea of learning to understand how other people make decisions:

- How long have you been working there?
- What did you do before that?
- What caused you to pursue this avenue of work?
- How is your job the same or different than you originally anticipated?
- What's the next step in your career?

Questions, questions, questions.

Have you ever asked someone how they got to where they are today only to find their journey is not only uncommon but also a complete surprise to you?

When I started asking questions and began listening to how others asked me questions, I improved my ability to get others to open up. That became a skill and later a habit that has helped me throughout my career.

What became evident to me was that many people ended up in a career that started in another field entirely! Learning what people went through on their career journey was fascinating to me. I learned so much about perseverance and being open-minded to opportunities that came along. I learned that being curious and inquisitive could actually be a personal strength.

In their book *Power Questions*, Andrew Sobel and Jerold Panas stated, "Good questions challenge your thinking. They reframe and redefine the problem. They throw cold water on our most dearly held assumptions, and force us out of our traditional thinking. They motivate us to learn and discover more. They remind us of what is most important in our lives."[5]

Your journey to connect with others who can be impact players in your own life starts when you look beyond yourself. There is a perspective out there that is greater than you can possibly grasp on your own. But hang on! Once you start down this path, your life will never be the same again.

In the next two chapters I will define the roles and responsibilities that are part of the building blocks for putting together your own personal Board of Directors. Then I will lay out the road map for you as you learn to climb to new heights in your personal and professional development.

▲

"The significant problems we face cannot be solved at the same level of thinking we were at when we created them."

--Albert Einstein--

CHAPTER 1
Highlights

- Just because you started out on your own doesn't mean you have to keep going that way.

- You get to decide how you respond to whatever life throws at you.

- Making a change starts with you.

- It's time to consider a new way of thinking to get where you want to go.

- No one can live your life for you. This is your life, and it's up to you to go where you want to go and dream what you want to dream.

- Begin to think bigger! If your primary counselors are Me, Myself, and I, you're not thinking big enough!

CHAPTER 2

MAKE IT PERSONAL

"Time is the most valuable coin in your life. You and you alone will determine how that coin will be spent. Be careful that you do not let other people spend it for you."

--*Carl Sandburg*--

Being raised in Minnesota, the land of 10,000 lakes, had many advantages; however, growing up in a big family meant that real road trips were out of the question. Squeezing 11 people into the family sedan to go to Grandma's house was adventure enough for my parents. The road less traveled was really a road not traveled growing up, and I realized travel would be an adventure I had to find on my own—or with a friend.

My best friend, Joel, and I decided to discover life beyond Minnesota. Right out of high school, we took our inaugural trip together up into Canada. After 10 days, we realized the scenery was nice but still too similar to home. It was a fun journey, but like skiing on small hills in the winter in Minnesota, hiking around hills and bluffs in lower Ontario and Manitoba lacked a certain vertical perspective.

When we realized after that first camping trip we could survive spending 12–14 days together "roughing it," Joel and I upped the ante on our second trip to take our next adventure to new heights—the Rocky Mountains. Wading through maps and brochures supplied by the tourism bureaus in Canada, Montana, and Colorado (no internet back then!), we decided to start in the middle and chose Glacier National Park in northwestern Montana. We would experience more challenging hiking, but we'd avoid battling any extreme elements.

▲

A New Perspective

We hit the road for Montana the next summer and experienced a change in scenery that would change us forever.

As we drove west across the plains of North Dakota and into eastern Montana, we were able to see across the horizon for what seemed like hundreds of miles. That was so new and unique to us. The flat, wide-open spaces were simple yet beautiful. We had never really seen anything like it.

Then it happened. On the horizon, we could see an uneven pattern emerge in the distance. Like two little boys knowing that something wonderful was coming, we got more and more excited as we continued our westward drive. The mountains slowly got larger across the horizon, and even though we were still hours away, it was as if we were watching an event unfold in time-lapse photography.

This was new. This was mind-blowing. Even when we discussed it recently, we still remember it vividly all these years later. No amount of pictures can substitute for actually being there. Watching the horizon transform before our very eyes was nothing short of spectacular.

And hiking the Rocky Mountains was unparalleled in our lives up to that point. We were just a couple of kids from the Midwest looking for an adventure, and we found it.

▲

First Time

We've all had experiences for the first time that opened our minds and expanded our understanding and even changed our perspective. No one can tell you what something might be like and expect it to have the same effect on you as you actually doing it.

Your experience is your own. No one else can make it any more personal for you. This is up to you. It's your life opportunity to get out of your comfort zone and think differently. Whether that means thinking bigger or simply outside the box, changing your thinking about what you want—what you really want—is an important and courageous step in your journey to grow beyond yourself.

▲

Purpose of a Personal Board of Directors

If you have ever been part of an organization that had a traditional Board of Directors in structure and in roles, that is not what I'm talking about here. A traditional Board of Directors is designed to provide governance to an organization. They make decisions and set policy for the betterment of the organization's interests.

I am simply using the term "Board of Directors" to point out there is a team that is gathered to serve as coaches and mentors to direct you toward making better decisions for your life. It is a "personal" Board of Directors designed by you, built by you, and chosen by you for your own personal growth and development. You define their roles. They will serve as an additional set of eyes, ears, and minds that will listen to you, ask questions to clarify and understand, and potentially offer suggestions or advice from their own experiences.

Here is an important truth about the purpose of building your personal Board of Directors: *This is not a club.* You are not looking for people to agree with you. This is not a gathering of your best friends or co-workers.

This is a strategic team of mentors, counselors, and advisors. The makeup of your board should consist of a variety of different people in order for you to expand your perspective and give you the broadest view of whatever it is you are facing. I personally believe everyone should have a personal Board of Directors made up of at least three to five members.

You are looking for people from various backgrounds with whom you will develop a trust relationship. This will allow you to open yourself up to the wisdom of others and see beyond yourself.

Word of caution: This is not as easy as it sounds. As a matter of fact, many will say this is what they want, yet few actually move to the point of being open to others because they are afraid ... to trust ... to be honest ... to be vulnerable ... to be humble ... to be transparent.

To gain the most value from something, you have to give it your best. Having your own personal Board of Directors is no different. Remember you are putting together a team to help you grow beyond your own capabilities. Now is the time to be strategic as you seek to expand your vision beyond your own perspective.

The purpose of having a personal Board of Directors is to expand your perspective by learning from the wisdom, insight, and experience of others in order to make quality decisions for your personal and professional life.

When you operate on your own, you remain on the ground level in your ability to see things for what they are *and* for what they could be. Growth will come when you open yourself up to others. Finding partners for the journey does not mean you are relinquishing your power or giving up your decision-making. It means you will improve the quality of your decisions as you gain new perspectives through the wisdom and insight from others.

This should be an encouragement to you and a confidence boost! You will form greater conviction about the decisions you make because gaining others' perspectives will allow you to scale to new heights and see things with greater clarity.

To make sure we are on the same page when it comes to defining roles, we will need to confirm our understanding, so we are all working from the same definitions and the same initial perspective.

▲

Mentor

According to Dictionary.com, a mentor is: *a wise and trusted counselor or teacher.*[1] The key words in this definition give us a clue to embrace as we think about who our mentors should be. Who has wisdom and experience and is willing to share it? Who can I build a trust relationship with? How do I go about establishing that relationship of trust with someone as a mentor?

Do you remember a teacher or coach who you liked or believed in or trusted when you were growing up? What were the characteristics that led you to feel that way? Was it the way they engaged with you or challenged you or encouraged you? Was it their teaching style that made them stand out to you?

The term "mentor" comes from ancient Greece and the story of the son of Odysseus, named Telemachus, who had a guardian named Mentor. It was Mentor's responsibility to teach and train Telemachus about how life worked and what it meant to become a man, while his father, Odysseus, was off fighting the Trojan War.[2]

This pattern of acting as a father-figure of sorts is a clear example of the role of a mentor—someone who influences and guides another for their growth and development.

I don't believe that all your mentors should necessarily be older than you. It is really a matter of what type of experience you are looking for. You're looking for people who have particular knowledge or have done something that will bring value and perspective to your thinking, which you couldn't gain on your own.

▲

Mentee

The definition of a mentee is: *a person guided by a mentor.*[3]

Notice the key word is "guided." It's not about being told what to do. It's not about having no say in the strategy or course to take. As a matter of fact, it's more about how to listen and gather insight from others you invite into your life.

Seeking to understand is much more important than telling someone what to do. If a mentor is someone who is wise and trusted as a counselor or teacher, then you need to assume the role of a student. This is how you put yourself in a position to receive from others. This is where it starts, and it is how you break the habit of going it alone.

Remember, it's not a sign of weakness to put yourself in a position to be taught by others. Some may even consider this to be a sign of strength. Because when you open yourself up to the wisdom and experience of others, you are seeking to grow and get stronger in areas where you currently lack or have a limited perspective.

A mentor/mentee relationship is about guidance, not governance. Whether you are mentoring or being mentored, you must keep in mind that you are in a relationship that has its purpose in sharing openly with one another. Expanding your perspective and asking clarifying questions is at the heart of the matter. It's about gathering from the wisdom and experience of others in order to make better, more informed decisions for your own life.

Leadership development is no different in that you are preparing yourself mentally to trust others to guide you and you must take action to grow in leadership. It is not merely a mind exercise. This is a partnership built on trust and honesty not common in today's world.

▲

Respect Key Relationships

In forming your personal Board of Directors, you are doing more than seeking advice from others; you are asking them to participate in an open, honest, transparent, and trusting relationship. I recommend that in the formation of your board, you keep in mind your own primary relationships, such as with your spouse. For example, it was important to me to honor my wife by not putting myself in a position to enter a relationship at a deeper level of transparency with another woman. That is why I have chosen to only invite other men to be on my personal board. The people closest to you will support your interactions with your board when they see that you are respecting their needs and prioritizing your relationship with them.

▲

Make It Your Own

Years after my last trip with Joel to the Rocky Mountains, singer and songwriter, Dan Fogelberg, came out with his "High Country Snows" album. It was a down-home, bluegrass-style recording that had as its closing song an anthem that revealed the importance of perspective that really resonated with me. The song is called, "The Higher You Climb," and I encourage you to pause and reflect as you read the following lyrics:

> *The higher you climb, the more that you see.*
> *The more that you see, the less that you know.*
> *The less that you know, the more that you yearn.*
> *The more that you yearn, the higher you climb.*[4]

▲

In order to make it personal you have to take it personally.

This is your journey.

This is your life.

I have observed friends and colleagues who had kept their heads down as they climbed the corporate ladder, and found the destination was not what they had thought it was going to be! Having been so focused on climbing, they had taken their eyes off of where they were going. This left them confused—their ideas of what it would be like at the top didn't line up with their reality.

Have you been there?

Have you ever lost sight of the big picture?

Or have you ever focused so hard on the big picture you failed to take care of the basics along the way or even enjoy the journey?

It's as if when you look up you can see where you want to go but you keep losing traction as you climb. You end up so focused—either on what's at hand or what's ahead—you struggle to navigate to the end result you were seeking.

In his book *Monday Morning Leadership*, David Cottrell tells the story of a manager named Jeff Watters and his mentor, Tony Pearce. Jeff was in a management position at his company, and he was struggling in a number of areas, so he went in search of what to do about it. He sought out a conversation with Tony, an old family friend and well-respected member of the community, for advice. What he got was a lesson in leadership that changed his life.

Jeff started out by asking Tony for a few minutes of his time to get some advice on his situation at work. Tony listened and then offered to work with him if Jeff would commit to two things:

> *"1. Tony said that he was not interested in helping solve my problems. He was interested in helping me become a better person and leader and that would require spending some significant time together. If I would commit to meeting with him every Monday morning for eight weeks, he would be glad to help.*
>
> *2. Tony also asked me to commit to teach others the lessons and experiences he would be sharing with me. He said none of my problems were unique and that others could learn from my experiences."*[5]

Tony's requirements provide an example of a powerful and strategic offer and demonstrate the timeless truth of what being a mentor really is all about. Notice that in the first commitment Tony clarified that he was not interested in solving Jeff's problems; he was not attempting to be a prescriber. He wanted to be a counselor and adviser, a true mentor. Tony wanted to teach Jeff how to be his own man and enhance his ability to make quality decisions.

Tony's weekly pattern consisted of asking a series of clarifying questions, followed by a review of the actions steps that Jeff had taken during the previous week. He then provided guidance and offered additional questions for Jeff to ponder in order to identify his own action items for the coming week.

Also notice that based on Jeff's needs, Tony suggested a specific schedule—every Monday morning for eight weeks. This is not a requirement and every mentor/mentee relationship will be different based upon what you are seeking and how you want to engage.

Making it personal does not mean keeping it to yourself!

The reality of that statement takes on new clarity when we look at what authors Paul Batz and Tim Schmidt have to say in their book *What Really Works*. They share the importance of what they call the Seven Fs: Faith, Family, Finances, Fitness, Friends, Fun, and Future.

Batz and Schmidt say, "One of the simplest lessons we've learned from our efforts to share the Seven Fs insights of others is the positive power of mentorship. We've repeatedly heard from people who openly credit their success to what they've learned from mentors—and what they've learned by mentoring. One of life's greatest joys is finding ways for people to succeed together!"[6]

What a great confirmation of the power of mentoring and being mentored!

▲

A New Way of Thinking

So, how do you get started?

How do you discover what you really want?

How will you confirm what you want as you climb?

Let's take a look at a new way of thinking. Rather than being bound and determined to "get there," let's look at markers along the way that will help evaluate your progress and the clarity of your path.

Making good decisions, even when they're hard, shouldn't come based solely on emotion or circumstance. They should be grounded in sound advice. Where many people fail is when they randomly choose who they talk to because of convenience rather than sound strategy. When this is the case, the conversation tends to be geared more toward seeking approval for your ideas or position rather than discussing the options and considering all the aspects of the issue before you.

Remember the goal here is not only about making decisions; it's about helping you make *quality* decisions for your life. Making a decision shouldn't be based upon someone else's perspective or opinion. It should be based on a discussion with them about *your* circumstances. It should not be as simple as their answer to one question. You're not looking for agreement without perspective, nor are you looking for someone to simply say "yes" to your ideas.

The role of a mentee follows this pattern:

- Ask for advice based on the discussion around your questions.
- Ask for their perspective on any experience they have had in handling this type of situation in the past.
- Ask them about their process and what questions they asked themselves and others.
- Seek specific examples.
- Ask clarifying questions.
- TAKE NOTES!

When meeting with my mentors, I go into every counseling conversation with a prepared series of questions. The pattern that has worked best for me over the years has been to examine each of the following elements or steps:

- Share the details of my current situation.
- Offer my initial thoughts on possible courses of action or identify any specific barriers.
- Engage by asking and answering specific questions. Enjoy this time of dialogue and take notes!
- Process my new-found perspective and confirm my understanding of what was shared.
- Take what I have learned and begin to strategize my nest steps. I need to be as specific as possible—this will drive me to take action!
- Sample Questions:
- What am I missing?
- What strategies would you suggest I pursue?
- Who else should I consider talking to?
- What other questions do I need to consider?

I may need a response or perspective on the spot, or I may ask them to think about my circumstances and get back to me within a given time. Either way, they typically follow up by asking me clarifying questions to ensure they are responding to the real need and not a perceived need.

▲

Be Intentional

Being intentional makes all the difference when engaging your personal Board of Directors. Don't miss out on the opportunity to gain wisdom and insight from their experiences.

It's important they don't feel as though they are wasting their time with you, or worse yet, you're wasting their time. If you walk away from a meeting with an action plan, make sure to tell them about the outcome. Keep them updated and engaged, especially when any advice they previously shared helped you navigate successfully through your circumstances.

If you come back to a follow-up meeting and haven't done what you said you were going to do in the previous meeting, then you should strongly consider rescheduling unless there are new circumstances that are causing you to question the action plan.

Be honest! This is a relationship built on trust and it should always work both ways. Build trust. Earn trust. Give trust. Make trust the cornerstone of your relationship with your individual board members and you will never be sorry. You don't need to impress your mentors. Just be honest.

Resolve in your own mind that you are building your personal Board of Directors for your own long-term benefit. This strategy will help you navigate in ways you could not have imagined in the past. Our ability to grow will not be like addition—adding one thing to another—it will be more like multiplication. Your ability to make quality decisions will start to grow at a faster rate, and your results will multiply as you become smarter and stronger in your leadership development.

Climbing the Rockies was pivotal in my journey and in my understanding of the importance of perspective. Once I realized that I couldn't see what I couldn't see, what was outside of my vision or beyond what was in front of me, it made the value in seeing things from a new perspective that much more powerful and amazing.

In the next chapter, we will examine how a roadmap can help you navigate your way to new heights and gain a peak perspective. We will also look at the definitions and specific roles that you will want to have as part of your team and then introduce the five key steps to building your own personal Board of Directors.

▲

"Your greatest possession is the twenty-four hours you have directly ahead of you. How will you spend it?"

--John C. Maxwell--

CHAPTER 2
Highlights

- When you choose to make it personal, you add fuel to the fire inside of you. Remember your experience is your own, and no one else can make it any more personal for you.

- The purpose of a personal Board of Directors is to expand your perspective by learning from the wisdom, insight, and experience of others in order to make quality decisions for your personal and professional life.

- Important truth—this is not a club! You are building a strategic team of mentors, counselors, and advisors.

- A mentor is defined as: *a wise and trusted counselor or teacher.*

- A mentee is defined as: *a person guided by a mentor.*

- Making this personal means you get to make this process your own. This is your journey. This is your life.

- Be intentional and be honest with yourself and the process of moving toward building your own personal Board of Directors.

CHAPTER 3
YOUR ROADMAP

"Without vision you can't see yourself or your world clearly."

--Kary Oberbrunner--

Knowing the general direction you're going—or where you want to go—is important. If you move in the direction of where you want to go, you're bound to get closer to your destination. Have you ever gotten into your car to go on an errand, and after driving for a few blocks, you realize you don't remember what errand you are running or where you are supposed to be going?

Every traveler knows the importance of having a map to chart your course. Believe it or not, this even applies when you want to *feel* your way across the country. You still need to decide what direction you're heading and whether or not there is a deadline to get where you are going.

Strong leaders always have a plan. They don't make decisions in isolation. They surround themselves with others who provide input to help guide their thinking. The best leaders will typically gather the data and ask for input from others before making the final decision. This ensures that the final decision is an informed one. It doesn't mean they won't make mistakes. It means the team works together to help in the process and then continues to work together to make adjustments as changes take place along the way.

Quality decisions are made with a team approach. This is your game plan—your road map.

Whether you are looking for key input for your personal or professional life, the same rules still apply.

Build your team.

Engage your team.

Ask your team.

Listen to your team.

Learn from your team.

Make quality decisions.

▲

Your Road, Your Map

In his book *Never be the Same*, Mark LeBlanc shares a story of his own experience and personal challenge in making the pilgrimage to *Camino de Santiago* in Spain. After hearing a friend share about making this journey, LeBlanc became captivated by the little *five-hundred-mile* trek across Northern Spain. Once he decided to make it personal and put it on his calendar, he finally set out on this hike up and over the Pyrenees mountain range that divides France and Spain.

As with any physical challenge, there usually comes a point of personal examination or battle over why you are putting yourself through the rigors of your journey. Such was the personal battle LeBlanc faced as he started out on his walk up and over the mountains. At one point early on, he was exhausted as he climbed upward and the air got thinner. When he felt like he could go no farther that day, he gratefully found himself within a few kilometers of the hostel where he could get a meal and some rest.

As he discussed the day's journey with other walkers over dinner, he met a woman from England who had been taking this challenge on at an entirely different pace. He asked her if she had any advice for him, and she said, "Mark, you can always take another step. No matter how tired you are, no matter how miserable you are, you can always take another step."[1]

Those words rang out for LeBlanc on the spot and he found a new level of motivation he didn't have before.

Has that ever happened to you? Have you ever heard some inspiring words or witnessed a feat that captivated you? Have you ever been motivated by an amazing performance, powerful talk or unique experience?

The lesson here is that when others share their experiences, and encouragement—their perspective—it can have a powerful impact on you. That's the value of gaining new perspective from insights others are willing to share with you.

As you look ahead on your own journey, you may be saying to yourself, "That's fine for you, but my situation is different." The beauty of this map is found in the fact that it only serves as a guide. It is designed to be customized by *you* to meet *your* needs. This will resonate with you and take off in the direction you want it to go when you begin to engage and open yourself up to others.

It's not my intent to tell you, "This worked for me. If you just do what I did, it will work for you too!" I am not prescribing a solution. I am simply providing a guide to help you design the roadmap that works best for you.

No one walks where you walk and sees what you see exactly as you do, which is why it's important for you to customize your own map. Use this simple template and customize it to your needs.

The greatest value in building your own personal Board of Directors is found in you. It's found in the way you grow your perspective and gain confidence by listening and learning from the wisdom and insight of others—from those you have chosen to bring along in your journey. Your map is your customized plan for explosive growth. It will guide you to make quality decisions and prepare you to take on new opportunities. It will also help you navigate through any challenge you face knowing you are not alone.

▲

Keys to Expand Your Perspective

I want you to know you can do it. You can grow in ways you couldn't previously imagine. As you think about your desired future state, believe you can get there. Start now to imagine having a team that guides you to make better decisions and helps you navigate your way toward your desired destination.

We all have the benefit of hindsight. We can look back at situations from our past and realize things could have worked out differently if we had made a different decision ... asked for advice ... listened to others ... waited for answers instead of jumping to conclusions ... taken action, etc.

I believe everyone has the ability to climb to new heights. I believe it so much I wrote this book to help you become the very best you can be. This continues to be an amazing journey for me and I want the same for you. When leaders grow and develop with wisdom, insight, and discernment, impact is made in the market-place. The plan I developed years ago has made all the difference in my ability to make quality decisions and grow and lead with impact. It has made all the difference for me in my journey. Looking back, I knew I couldn't succeed only with wishing about how I wanted my life to be in the future. I needed a plan. After learning and understanding the importance of building my own personal Board of Directors, I put together a five-step plan that simplified the process and gave me a road map to follow. This map has worked for me for years, and I believe it can also work for you when you customize it to your needs.

My journey started when I committed to thinking beyond myself. I set out to search for others to be part of my personal Board of Directors. Building this team would take a game plan that would produce a consistency I could use throughout the search process.

▲

C-L-I-M-B to new heights and gain an amazing perspective

Whenever you begin moving ahead, you want to remember it starts out one step at a time. When you desire to climb to new heights you don't leap to the top of the mountain. You have to navigate your way up, step-by-step. This is exactly how I looked at my plan to develop a personal Board of Directors. I put together a format that made sense and would guide me incrementally to where I wanted to go. Hiking up a mountainside sometimes meant I had to go sideways in order to gain new ground. It wasn't always a vertical path. There were times when I had to move horizontally across the mountain to find better terrain before I could continue vertically. Each step along the way was important as I considered both my current circumstances and where I ultimately wanted to end up.

Here are the five steps that allowed me to think beyond myself and build a team of mentors. Each step is important and should be approached in sequence, just like climbing a mountain.

C-L-I-M-B is a step-by-step process that will allow you to be purposeful and intentional in developing your personal Board of Directors.

1. **C**reate a New Mindset

    This goes beyond just changing your thinking. To stop flying solo, you first have to decide you want to break the habit. Once you do, you will benefit greatly when you take action and create and build a new mindset—one with lasting value and sets you on a new path.

2. Look for Influence

   Before you invite someone to join your personal
   Board of Directors, you need to examine the
   type of influence they will bring to the relationship. Not everyone will qualify to be on your
   board. This is not about gathering a team of
   your closest friends. You are looking for a level
   of influence that positively impacts your ability
   to see what's ahead and guides you in navigating
   through the challenges and opportunities you
   face. Don't underestimate the power of influence. It is the key factor in your ability to make
   quality decisions.

3. Invest in Right Relationships

   As you engage with those individuals you are
   considering inviting to join your personal board,
   remember the first step is your own humility.
   The investment comes when you are willing to
   be honest, open, and transparent with others.
   Building these relationships is a two-way street.
   You want to develop long-term relationships in
   order to maximize the value of having a personal
   Board of Directors.

4. Make the Call

   The decision is yours. Who you invite to be on
   your board is completely your call. You need to
   be diligent and specific in how and who you
   choose to be on your board. This is your personal
   board. This is where you get to decide who's in.

The right people on your board will make all the difference in the type of value you gain and growth you will experience. Choose wisely.

5. **Be** the Difference

    One of the greatest values in learning from the wisdom, insight, and experience of others is your ability to grow into the leader you were meant to be. You didn't get to the top by yourself. As you learn and grow along the way, you will become motivated to be the difference in the lives of others. It's time to share the benefits you have received from your own board. This is the most rewarding step in the process.

Following this path will help you raise your game to new heights. This path will deliver an enhanced perspective and immeasurable value to you. It will lead you in building your own team of mentors and develop personally as a leader of others. We will look at each of these steps in depth over the next five chapters to help you navigate your way up the path to a higher view in order to realize and achieve your own peak perspective.

▲

"All you need is the plan, the road map, and the courage to press on to your destination."

--Earl Nightingale--

CHAPTER 3
Highlights

- If you move in the direction of where you want to go you're bound to get closer to your destination.

- Strong leaders always have a plan. They don't make decisions in isolation.

- Quality decisions are made with a team approach.

- This is your game plan—your road map.

- No one walks where you walk and sees what you see exactly as you do, which is why it's important for you to customize your own map.

- Your map is your customized plan for explosive growth.

- **C-L-I-M-B** is a step-by-step guide that will allow you to be purposeful and intentional in developing your personal Board of Directors.

  o **C**reate a New Mindset

  o **L**ook for Influence

  o **I**nvest in Right Relationships

  o **M**ake the Call

  o **B**e the Difference

PART TWO

SOLUTION

DEVELOP YOUR PERSONAL BOARD OF DIRECTORS

Peak
Perspective

Be the Difference

Make the Call

Invest in Right Relationships

Look for Influence

Create a New Mindset

JimZugschwert.com

CHAPTER 4
CREATE A NEW MINDSET

"It marks a big step in your development when you come to realize that other people can help you do a better job than you could do alone."

--Andrew Carnegie--

Have you ever changed your mind? Have you ever thought of another way to do something? Have you ever chosen an alternate route on your GPS?

Creating a new mindset is not only about changing your mind. It's about metamorphosis—transformational change. It's the kind of change that starts from the inside out and brings about an entirely new way of thinking and doing. It's about creating new habits and patterns in your life that will bring about better results and greater possibilities.

In his book *Good to Great*, Jim Collins discusses the key threads that drove transformative change and caused companies to move from being good companies to becoming great ones. In seeking to understand the transformation and the sustainability that resulted in enduring, great companies, the studies shed light on some key characteristics in the transition from good to great that surprised Collins and his team.

One of their key discoveries is worth looking at as we discuss the importance of creating a new mindset. One of the measured results showed the importance of do's and don'ts. According to Collins, "The good-to-great companies did not focus principally on what to do to become great; they focused equally on what *not* to do and what to *stop* doing."[1]

Notice the real change happened when there was a concerted effort to focus on what to do (action plan and new behaviors) AND what not to do (avoid) AND what to stop doing (eliminate). For you this holistic view of your circumstances can be a powerful way to identify what to change and how to change.

The fundamentals of change are found in simple steps, not in complex formulas! You need to get right to the basics and take them on one step at a time and *then* build from there. Transformation will come as you build step-by-step toward your future goals.

▲

Getting Started

Understanding you can't go it alone is only the beginning. Real change doesn't happen until you decide to act in creating a new mindset. It's not just thinking about the idea and agreeing with it. Action is required.

You need to do something about it to change it from an idea to a new reality.

What turned out to be the simplest way for me to approach the idea of creating a new mindset was to break it down to four fundamentals. Once I zeroed in on these fundamentals, I was on the road to creating a new mindset that would lead me to greater purpose and understanding.

▲

Four Fundamentals for Creating a New Mindset

Creating a new mindset starts with these four fundamentals:

1. Expand your perspective;

2. Make a decision;

3. Establish an action plan;

4. Follow through.

Let's look at each one independently.

Expand your perspective: Once I realized I needed to stop going it alone in all areas of my life, I looked to others to gain new insight. For me, expanding my perspective meant deliberately looking at the lives of others and being intentional as I engaged with them. I didn't begin asking random questions; I asked specific questions regarding their family, business, faith, passions, balance, and even who was mentoring *them*.

Make a decision: I began to see a pattern of connections to others in leadership that helped these people become successful. They were not alone in their thinking, and regularly relied on key people in their lives to make sure they were thinking through the issues they were facing before making a decision. I could see a real benefit, an actual advantage in what they were doing and how it was making a significant difference in their lives.

You must first recognize the way you have been doing things has not gotten you to where you thought you wanted to go. Also, consider this: in getting to where you are today, you are able to recognize some of the limitations around you that you hadn't seen or considered before. It's time to decide to do things differently.

Establish an Action Plan: Creating a new mindset starts internally. It starts with revising your way of thinking and reviewing your daily habits. The most effective strategy in accomplishing your long-term goals starts with what you do daily. Thoughts become actions, actions become habits, and habits become character. Start with the basics and stick to it. Your daily habits will build the pattern for transformation. You are not waving a magic wand. You are charting a course for a new adventure. This journey will bring an expanded perspective that will empower you to make better decisions and move forward with new purpose in your life.

Follow Through: Once you establish an action plan, you must then take action. Once you begin to move toward your goal, you want to remain committed to it all the way to the finish line. Don't stop when things get tough. Don't give up when it seems too much to handle. Keep going and follow through. As with any action plan, you must be determined to move and stay at it. The ability to follow through with your decision is critical to your success.

▲

Personal Example

As an avid golfer, I often see life's situations from the perspective of the game. In the game of golf, as in life, impact is most effective toward your intended target when you start with the right setup (grip and alignment), takeaway (backswing), impact (striking the ball), and finish (in balance and under control). These steps will bring about consistent performance toward your desired outcome (hole).

This example can easily be converted to the four fundamentals above. Start with the right setup (determine to *Expand your Thinking*), takeaway (*Make a Decision*), impact (*Establish an Action Plan*), and finish (*Follow Through*). When performed in the right sequence, you will be on your way toward your desired outcome (*Goal*).

▲

Pulse Check

Where you are today is the result of the decisions you have made and have not made in the last ten years. What many fail to acknowledge is the decision to wait or do nothing is still a decision that produces results, which rarely turn out to be the results you were after.

Though often forgotten or overlooked as the key to accomplishing your long-term strategies, it's important to recognize the best measure of how you are doing and where you are going is found in your daily habits! Changing your mindset or your thinking starts with reviewing the things you normally do every day. If you are constantly trying to take on everything by yourself, you need to stop.

Another way to think about it would be to start with examining where you have been, where you are, and where you want to go. Move beyond thinking about what it is you want to do in order to facilitate change. Thinking alone may often be no more than wishing. Taking action that brings about change will start you down a new path.

Here's an effective exercise for making a change. It starts with examining the following perspectives: where I've been, where I am, and where I'm going within the context of What, How, and Why.

Looking back:
    What have I been doing?
    How have I been doing it?
    Why have I been doing it?

Looking at today:
    What do I need to change?
    How will I change?
    Why do I need to change?

Looking forward:
    What do I want to do?
    How will I do it?
    Why do I want to do it?

These are all great questions and a great place to start the process for changing. Looking back shows the picture of what has and hasn't happened. Reflecting on what might have been is not what you're going for here. There is no room for "would-a, could-a, should-a" in your thinking. That is a waste of time. Accept that where you have been was the result of choices you made with the information you had at the time. It's best to keep it as a point of reference and no more.

Next, comes your current state—a time for self-examination. Focus on what you are doing and what you need to change to gain a different outcome. You have the power to choose a new result. Start to think about what you want within the framework of what you need to change.

Once you examine your current state, think about what you hope for in the future. What do you want to do? How will you do it? Why is that important to you? These questions will get you to think forward and then identify how to make changes now to move toward that desired future state.

▲

Why

Another effective approach to consider comes from Simon Sinek. In his book *Start With Why*, Sinek addresses the fault in choosing what to do and how to do it without first considering why. His whole premise revolves around a company's shift to understanding why they are doing something, making a change, starting a new path, etc., before contemplating the "what" and the "how." He uses a visual of three rings—like a target—with an inner ring, middle ring, and outer ring. He calls it the "golden circle."[2] Most companies start their strategic approach with what they do, then how they do it, and finish up with why they do what they do. If you consider that *What* is the outer ring, *How* is the middle ring and *Why* is the center, most companies approach their strategy from the outside in. Sinek makes it clear that the highly successful companies work from the inside out. They identify why they do what they do—their purpose, cause or belief—and covey that message to their prospective customers. This tends to create loyal customers who resonate with the company's purpose and passion for why they do what they do.

I mention this idea because I believe this approach can also be effective in developing your personal strategy. I ask you to consider the idea of identifying your why first—your purpose, cause, or belief—to clarify your action plan based on that which is most important to you. Knowing your why will help you put the correct action plan together as you set out to create a new mindset. When you understand why you are doing something, it becomes easier and clearer for others to understand your motives, and their buy-in to where you are going gets locked in more quickly.

Once I realized I needed to change I was on my way. I knew if I wanted different results, I had to start with a fresh approach—a new mindset. For me, this simply meant I needed to examine why I was doing what I was doing. When my purpose became clearer to me, I could see the actions I needed to take and the things I needed to stop doing—like trying to do everything myself!

▲

Don't Go Solo

So often we strive with our own perspective as the only credible influence in our lives. We may take in other information, but most often we conclude our own ideas are correct or our method is the best approach. We are so easily deluded by our own lack of perspective.

It's time to recognize we must stop flying solo through life.

It's time to stop thinking we have all the answers.

It's time to understand we will need others in order for us to grow to our maximum potential.

It's time to create a new mindset.

Whether you are taking on a new job or responsibility or entering a new phase in your life, recognize you haven't been there before, and you don't know all the answers or even all the questions before you!

You will need the perspective of others to help guide your thinking. The perspective of others, especially those with applicable experience, can help you navigate the road ahead. If you are willing to open yourself up to others, you can gain new perspective by learning from their guidance and experience.

In his book *The Power of Purpose*, Richard J. Leider explains the plight most people feel as they search for meaning in their lives.

"If we had to name what makes life worth living, what gives it meaning and purpose, most of us would probably say it's the people we love. Relationships, along with work, are the core differences in quality of life at all ages. Whom we love and how we love them are in a way the fundamental reasons we get up in the morning."

Despite this fact, Leider notes that isolation is the number-one issue in many people's lives, and a sense of aloneness affects almost half of us. He concludes, "Busy lives can result in an abundance of acquaintances and a poverty of true friends."[3]

Living our lives in isolation doesn't really get us where we want to go. We need to start thinking differently to change our habits and patterns. This is an important step to pay attention to as we often find ourselves falling back into old habits when the pressure is on. If you have ever done the same things repeatedly while expecting different results, then you know why that action is considered a definition of insanity.

▲

The Fundamentals

It was the summer of 1961. Vince Lombardi, one of the greatest professional football coaches and leaders of men, stated the importance of fundamentals at the start of each season. It didn't matter that his team was in the championship game the year before and lost the lead and the game in the end. He chose to start training camp for the new season by focusing on the fundamentals. In his book, *When Pride Still Mattered: A Life of Vince Lombardi*, David Maraniss, describes the scene: "He began with the most elemental statement of all. 'Gentlemen,' he said, holding a pigskin in his right hand, 'this is a football.'"[4]

He looked at the new season as just that—new. No preconceived notions. No carryovers from the previous season. No reason to leap ahead.

He refused to look past the fundamentals some of their competition would ultimately take for granted. He went into detail about the small things, the common actions and steps necessary to have in place before he would begin to build on them. They were going to be the best at doing the fundamentals consistently.

This strategic response and plan for the new season became the foundation for winning five championships in the next seven years!

▲

The Importance of a Team (The Power of Partners)

The Apollo 13 mission to the moon in 1970 provides a prime example of the importance of a team. The challenges that occurred during this mission and the ultimate outcome showed how everyone had a role in bringing the astronauts home safely. It wasn't the captain or just the crew. It required the full participation of all members of the project, including scientists and engineers back home who had to think "outside the box" under the pressure of time and the consideration of the life and death of the astronauts.

Captain Jim Lovell and his crew launched from Earth on April 11, 1970, to follow in the footsteps of Neil Armstrong and walk on the moon again. Their space flight would take the crew on several life-threatening journeys throughout their time in the air and although they went *around* the moon, they never got to land on it because they were in survival mode as they made their attempt to return to Earth alive.

"Houston, we have a problem…" were the words uttered by Captain Lovell and heard round the world as they had determined, 22 hours into the flight, there had been some sort of on-board explosion.

It's easy to take for granted what is done behind the scenes in putting together a presentation or an event. We participate in the event itself and don't even consider the hours, days and weeks of planning it took to put something together to have an impact. Why is that? Why do we miss the hidden efforts of others?

It most often has to do with our own perspective, or lack of it. When we think in terms of our own experience we miss the fact that a team of others made our experience more enjoyable, valuable, and impactful.

In the case of the Apollo 13 crew, gathering a team of great minds together to plot a solution was critical to the success of the mission. It ended up being the difference between life and death. In the movie about this famed, fated flight, Ed Harris, played the role of Flight Director, Gene Kranz, who displayed words and behavior that spoke volumes about the power of partners working together to get the astronauts home alive. As he overheard a comment about this potentially being one of the greatest disasters in NASA history, he said, "With all due respect gentlemen, I believe this will be our finest hour!"[5]

Even though they didn't walk on the moon, the mission was considered a success from many perspectives because of the way everyone, in space and on the ground, worked together to bring the three astronauts home safely.

▲

Getting Beyond Yourself

There was a time when I was not as effective as I wanted to be and was unsure of what to do about it. I was floundering in my career and in my life. It appeared I was merely getting by and living day to day. I had fallen into the trap of giving very little thought to where I wanted to go or what I wanted to do. I needed to start thinking beyond myself.

How do I do that?

How do I move beyond the plateau of my own thinking?

Once I realized this plateau was the result of the limitations of my own thinking, I decided to look around and begin observing the lives of others to see if there was anything of value I could find for myself. I was amazed to find the more I observed others, the more my own limitations came into focus.

The first action step for me was deciding to become curious!

I wanted to do more than observe the lives of others. I wanted to know and understand their thinking and their strategies in decision making and how they went about connecting with others. This started with simply getting to know them. My old tendency was to tell others about me and all that was going on in my life. Being curious meant I had to stop telling and start asking.

I learned over time the importance of asking questions and then listening to understand. This was a monumental change for me. Sadly, I had the bad habit of asking a question, and then while someone else was responding to me, I was busy in my mind getting ready to tell them something else or tell them about me rather than listening to their response. I remember once hearing at a meeting the idea that leaders listen, they don't do all the talking. NEWSFLASH! This simple statement hit me loud and clear. Yet, as much as I loved that idea, it still took me some time to adopt it as a real habit.

Creating a new mindset is not like flipping a switch. It takes daily discipline to change your thinking. It takes daily discipline to put an action plan in motion.

A great example of creating a new mindset by changing one's thinking and putting a new action plan in place comes from the life of Ben Franklin.

In his book *How to Win Friends and Influence People*, Dale Carnegie describes how a young Ben Franklin was insolent, opinionated, and quick to put others in their place. He became so offensive he was driving others away from him and seemed to have no ability to make friends, only enemies.

One day, an older and wiser Quaker friend came alongside him and strongly suggested to Ben he change his ways in dealing with people. He was much too abrasive and critical, and as a result, his opinions were building barriers between himself and others.

Part of the remarkable nature of this transformation was the way in which Ben Franklin handled the smarting rebuke. Carnegie goes on to say it this way, "He was big enough and wise enough to realize it was true, to sense he was headed for failure and social disaster. So, he made a right-about-face. He began immediately to change his insolent, opinionated ways."

He went on to quote Franklin who shared his own perspective on why and how he made the change from arrogance to statesmanship.

> *"I made it a rule," said Franklin, "to forbear all direct contradiction to the sentiment of others, and all positive assertion of my own. I even forbade myself the use of every word or expression in the language that imported a fix'd opinion, such as 'certainly,' 'undoubtedly,' etc., and I adopted, instead of them, 'I conceive,' 'I apprehend,' or 'I imagine' a thing to be so or so, or 'it appears to me at present.' When another asserted something that I thought in error, I deny'd myself the pleasure of contradicting him abruptly, and showing immediately some absurdity in his proposition: and in answering I began by observing that in certain cases or circumstances his opinion would be right, but in the present case there appear'd or seemed to me some difference, etc. I soon found the advantage of this change in my manner; the conversations I engag'd in went on more pleasantly. The modest way in which I propose'd my opinions procurr'd them a readier reception and less contradiction; I had less mortification when I was found to be in the wrong, and I more easily prevail'd with others to give up their mistakes and join with me when I happened to be in the right."*[6]

Ben Franklin had developed a reputation as a great statesman because he was willing to change his argumentative and combative ways and learned to deal fairly with others, even those he disagreed with. He took the suggestions, changed his ways, and developed the ability to relate to others which earned him the opportunity to lead others. Through wise counsel, he became an invaluable man of influence at the founding of the United States.

His willingness to listen and apply the advice given caused Franklin to make some immediate changes through quality decisions and literally changed his place in history.

What history will you make in your own legacy?

What lasting value and influence can you share with generations?

What will you do to leave a lasting impact on the lives of others?

Begin to write a new chapter in your story by understanding your own reasons why you want to change and put an action plan in place to create a new mindset for your future.

▲

"Your mindset matters. It affects everything—from the business and investment decisions you make, to the way you raise your children, to your stress levels and overall well-being."

--Peter Diamandis--

CHAPTER 4
Highlights

- Creating a new mindset is not about changing your mind. It's about metamorphosis. It's about transformational change.

- It starts with these four fundamentals:

    o Expand your perspective

    o Make a decision

    o Establish an action plan

    o Follow through

- Where you are today is the result of the decisions you have made—or not made—in the last ten years.

- The best measure of where you're going and how you're doing is found in your daily habits.

- Examine where you've been, where you are, and where you're going.

- Consider identifying your *why* first. Knowing your why will help you put the correct action plan together.

- It's time to recognize you must stop flying solo through life.

- Start thinking beyond yourself.

- Become curious!

- What will you do to leave a lasting impact on the lives of others?

CHAPTER 5

LOOK FOR INFLUENCE

"We should not only use all the brains we have, but all that we can borrow."

--Woodrow Wilson--

Where you start is not where you finish. You get to decide the path to your outcomes. Your circumstances don't define you, you define your circumstances.

Throughout your life you have been under the influence—of others! It started in your growing-up years. During the first couple of decades, you were surrounded by key people. Whether they were your parents, family members, guardians, coaches, teachers, or even siblings and friends, you grew up with a level of influence that had an impact on you and shaped your perspectives.

Great memories may continue to shape your life today as you look back on the positive influences and fun adventures you had along the way. When looking back on your life, you may also find some of these influences were not so positive, yet they still had the ability to drive you toward or away from something. As you move through adulthood, the people who have influence and impact on your life usually change. Yet even now, all around you are people who have some form of influence on you: your spouse, boss, co-workers, friends, neighbors, children, or others.

As you build your personal Board of Directors, start looking strategically for new levels of influence you want to model in your life. It's important to remember you now have an opportunity to examine the evidence in someone else's life before allowing them to impart any significant influence on you. You're grown up now, so you get to choose who influences you!

In his book *The 21 Irrefutable Laws of Leadership*, John Maxwell defines leadership at its most basic state in a chapter titled, "The Law of Influence." He conveys a powerful truth by breaking down the complexities of leadership into a simple statement:

"The True Measure of Leadership is Influence— Nothing More, Nothing Less."[1]

In building your personal Board of Directors, you want to learn to recognize influencers. You want the people who can help refine your thinking and enhance your personal, vocational, or spiritual development by sharing their perspective and experience. Your team of mentors should be diverse in life experience, so each person brings a view or perspective to a situation that is different from yours and different from your other board members.

I am not suggesting you allow someone to have complete influence over you. That is not what you are after! You develop an understanding of influence as you observe how others lead and through how they add value to other people. Watch how they engage in conversations, how they ask questions, how they enfold others into a group, etc. This exercise is about you observing and recognizing how influence works. From the actions of others, you can begin to determine the level of leadership and influence you want to model to enhance your personal development. You want to use and understand influence appropriately. It's about adding value to others. That's how influence should play out: it's not a position of dominance. It's about giving.

▲

Leadership

In the book *The Go-Giver*, by Bob Burg and John David Mann, they discuss the value of a leader learning to be a giver. The book introduces a definition of influence rooted in the principle of giving to others: "Your influence is determined by how abundantly you place other people's interests first." The authors teach that if you "watch out for what other people need … you'll get what you need."[2]

We can all learn from the power of influence when we strive to take our eyes off ourselves and put them on others.

▲

The Value of Influence

Through trial and error, I have learned to look for characteristics of influence in others by observing key areas in their lives. For example, I look to those who have demonstrated leadership qualities in my industry or in the industry I am interested in learning about. I look for specific examples where they address my areas of interest or where I need to develop so I can adopt their wisdom into my own strategies.

When I began developing my board, I looked for strategic thinkers. I would observe—directly or through conversations with them—how they responded when a circumstance came up, which had a direct impact on them or on those around them. I would ask them questions about the process, the pitfalls, and what they would consider doing differently in the future.

When it comes to the value of influence, you are not only looking for credentials, you are also looking for a relationship! This is your long-term plan. You can only embrace the influence of your board members when you have a real relationship with them. Their credibility with you will be enhanced by the fact that you are connected by a trust relationship based on openness and honesty.

On my personal Board of Directors, I have individuals who are highly aware of their circumstances and are effective in living strategically in the present. Their perspective is fresh, alive, and focused on having daily impact on those around them. One individual is also highly effective in regularly thinking about the future state of things. His influence and leadership are found not only in thinking about where we are today but also considering where we are going to go and how we are going to get there. The perspective of looking forward was an area of weakness for me, and his influence has helped expand my thinking beyond today.

I am looking for leadership qualities and characteristics that will teach me how to have impact in key relationships in my life—my spouse, children, friends, colleagues, neighbors, and community—in that order! I am looking for someone who can help me be a better husband, father, friend, co-worker, community member, and citizen.

For your board, look at the areas in your life that are important to you and seek out people who have the potential to expand your perspective in those areas. Then set up a time to get together with them. Before you can decide whether or not you want to invite them to be on your board, you'll need to spend some time with them. Be prepared to ask specific questions and monitor their responses. You want someone who is open and willing to share their wisdom and insight with you. I'll walk you through how to connect with them one at a time in chapter six.

You are looking for a person's demonstrated level of leadership; this will help you trust his or her ability to help you round out your abilities in areas where you want to grow.

As I look at the qualities and characteristics of the five people currently on my personal Board of Directors, I see a wide variety of experience and leadership values—personally, relationally, occupationally, and spiritually. I look to them all to stretch my thinking by expanding my perspective in all the applicable areas where they are strong. I encourage them to talk to me in ways that allow me to open my mind and stimulate my curiosity. This sets me up for growth in ways I could never accomplish on my own.

▲

Personal History — Flashback

When I was in my twenties, I was privileged to work for my dad in his building supply business. I was neither the oldest child nor even the oldest son in the family; however, I was the first college graduate. I was fairly convinced I knew what needed to be done and was fully capable of handling anything that came my way.

Gratefully, my dad saw it differently. He understood the importance of experience, and he realized he couldn't be my only mentor in life—even though my desk was right outside his office. He made a strategic move that had a tremendous impact on me throughout my twenties and thirties. Dad saw to it I got connected to three men from different companies and different industries.

A natural outcome from these mentors was the transition and development into a personal relationship beyond work. We started discussing life issues, marriage and family, vacations, hobbies, and other interests. Each of these men took me under his wing and helped me to grow and expand my professional and personal perspectives in ways that have had lifelong impact on me.

Through these relationships, I started to understand the importance and perspective of business in the framework of the bigger picture of life. We got to the point in our relationships where we could talk openly about our families and hobbies and things outside of the joys and pressures of work. They gave me insight into a thing called work-life balance. (It was also a benefit to me that all three of these men would use the platform of golf to connect with me!) It was through these activities, lunches, meetings, and events that I learned the importance of building relationships beyond the rigors of work.

Life is a people business! Building strong relationships and being willing to listen and discuss—without prescribing solutions—are highly effective ways of strengthening personal and professional bonds with others.

▲

Legacy

It wasn't until I was in my forties that I truly realized what my dad had modeled for me in my twenties. This realization and understanding had a profound impact on me, and I was grateful for the opportunity to share these observations with my dad before he passed away. We had fun reviewing the value these three guys brought to my life from my early days at his company.

We also reminisced about a couple of men he had connected me to when I was in my mid-thirties who had also helped years later to navigate the life transition for both of us in selling the family business in 1992— one of the most difficult decisions I had faced at that point in my life.

Having a team of mentors helped us all throughout this process and I will be forever grateful to my dad for showing me how to surround myself with people of influence to assist me in making great decisions and navigate through opportunities and challenges.

▲

Footprints

As you search for influence, consider the ground you are walking on. Have you ever noticed footprints when walking on a trail or a beach? What is your reaction? Rather than think someone beat you to this path or it's not a new adventure or new ground you're breaking if someone has already been here, consider this ... try being curious.

Who do they belong to? Who has gone before you on this path? What have they found? What have they learned? Would they be willing to share?

It's possible they could be someone worth talking to. Their experience may bring value to you as you march along this path. This level of curiosity can help you think beyond what you see in front of you and encourage you to reach out to those who have gone before you. As you look for influence, remember you are looking for those who have experience and would be willing to share with you as you develop a trust relationship with one another.

▲

"Trust is the glue of life. It's the most essential ingredient in effective communication. It's the foundational principle that holds all relationships."

--Stephen R. Covey--

CHAPTER 5
Highlights

- Your circumstances don't define you; you define your circumstances.

- "The true measure of leadership is influence—nothing more, nothing less."

- Providing effective influence in the lives of others is what true leaders are after. It's what separates a real leader from a manager.

- "Your influence is determined by how abundantly you place other people's interests first."

- When it comes to the value of influence, you are not just looking for credentials; you are also looking for a relationship!

- Look for leadership in the areas of your life that are important to you and look for people who have the potential to expand your perspective in those areas.

CHAPTER 6
INVEST IN RIGHT RELATIONSHIPS

"You can buy a man's time; you can buy his physical presence at a given place; you even can buy a measured number of his skilled muscular motions per hour. But you cannot buy enthusiasm ... you cannot buy loyalty ... you cannot buy the devotion of hearts, minds or souls. You must earn these."

--Clarence Francis--

You are on your way to climbing to new heights and approaching the peak as you consider which people to associate with in order to expand your perspective and develop leadership qualities and skills. Before you make the final decision as to who to invite to be on your personal Board of Directors, you need to understand what it means to make the proper investment in those relationships.

Investing in right relationships starts with where the responsibilities lie. When it comes to developing your personal Board of Directors, first identify the key people you want on your board, and then you must take responsibility to connect with them.

▲

Connect

The investment in building these relationships is not about a calendar or a schedule. It's not about your mentors coming to you asking to connect and follow up. As with any relationship, it takes engagement with one another to learn and grow to a deeper level of trust and understanding.

Investing in right relationships is your responsibility! You're climbing the mountain. You're seeking guidance. You're looking for a fresh perspective. The questions you ask may sound something like this:

Which path do I take when I come to a fork in the road?

How do I choose?

Which way do I go?

What are my options?

What do I do?

If you were here, what questions would you ask?

Investing is your responsibility. You drive the process. You engage those on your board at the level that meets your needs. You connect with people in a way that drives that investment value. You make the contact. You suggest the schedule.

Because this is up to you, I suggest you consider setting the parameters for contact and then give them the freedom to reach out to you periodically. Let them know they have the green light to check in from time to time, especially if they have something of interest they would like to share with you. Let them know you are always hungry for their perspective, experience, and even their thought process in how they handle issues in their own life circumstances.

How you want to engage and connect is up to you. This is your board. You decide how you'll connect—by phone, email, text, face-to-face, over coffee, or a meal. Know that you will likely engage each member differently based upon your needs and their proximity to you.

My personal Board of Directors consists of five men—three who live in the same metropolitan area as I do and two who live out of state. When and how I connect with them varies based on my needs and schedule and their needs and availability.

You will need to be flexible and accept how they connect based on what they bring to your relationship. You drive the level of investment and you also measure the value along the way. It's up to you to determine if a change to your board is necessary.

Of my current Board of Directors, three of them are original members and two are newer to this role as my needs have changed over the years. As stated previously, this is not a traditional corporate Board of Directors structure. I have never gathered all my board members together for a meeting! Some of my guys don't know each other at all, which is fine because they all fill different roles in my life.

I look for people to guide me in three areas: personal, professional, and spiritual. All of my board members don't fill every role. Each of them provides insight in at least two areas of my life, but it's not a requirement or minimum standard everyone has. Even if the specific experience is only in one area, if that provides great value, then it works for me.

▲

The Process of Engagement

Understanding how this process works is important to embrace before you make the final selection of your board members. Making a wise investment in these relationships is a strategic part of the plan and is vital to your ability to maximize the expansion of your perspective.

Whenever you face a significant decision in your life, you should reach out for a minimum of two perspectives. One is not enough! I can recall times when I received advice from one of my board members and felt like I had a total grasp on my situation only to find that in conversation with another board member, I realized there was more to my decision about what to do. Blending the advice by confirming multiple perspectives gave me a clearer view of how to move ahead.

Remember this is about expanding *your* perspective. You want a variety of feedback and questions from your board. You also get to decide what topics are significant to you. If you feel you want to bounce an idea off any of your board members regarding an opportunity or challenge that has come up in your life, then go ahead and connect. You may be surprised at how ready and willing they are to respond and engage with you knowing you thought enough of them to seek their perspective.

When you make the effort to invest in building relationships, both parties will prosper. You will learn from each other in ways that will surprise you both. The value that comes from connecting and sharing is illustrated through the biblical proverb, "As iron sharpens iron, a friend sharpens a friend."[1]

I caution you not to invest in relationships with others solely to get something from them. Look to grow together in a bond that will ultimately benefit both of you. The beauty of investing in right relationships is the added value that impacts both parties. It may be subtle, or it may be blatantly obvious. It will certainly develop naturally over time as you engage with one another.

The best way to connect with members of your board is to reach out and share what's going on in your life and address your questions. Important: This is not a time to dump all your problems on them expecting them to solve your problems for you.

This is—and should always be—about a conversation, which is why it's important for you to understand how and when you connect should be primarily driven by you. Take the lead. Reach out. Share your circumstance. Ask them specific questions. Listen to their experience and perspective and then answer their questions in the same way you expect them to answer you—honestly!

Your engagement can be as simple as the following:

"Hey, _____, I have a circumstance (situation, obstacle, opportunity) coming up I'd like to discuss with you. I have a couple of ideas I'd like to bounce by you and I also have a specific question for you.

When would be a good time in your schedule to talk on the phone or meet for coffee?"

Or

"Hi, _____, I just got surprised by (situation, obstacle, opportunity) and I need your advice. Let me know when you have a few minutes to talk. I'll need to decide (take action) by the end of the day tomorrow and I have a couple of questions for you. I will be around for the rest of the day. Call me when you are free or let me know when the best time would be to reach you. Thanks!"

Or

Hello, _____, this is _____. Would you be available to talk later today? I just lost my job. Please call me or let me know when you have some time to review what happened. I have some options I would like to discuss with you. Thanks."

▲

TIP: Be Prepared

Before you reach out and ask any of your board members to connect, make sure you've thought about your circumstances in advance. One of the best ways to set up the conversation is to lay out the issues you face and then provide them with your first impression on a possible strategy. Let them know what you're thinking. From there, you can ask your questions and then listen. This gives them the confidence and understanding to know you're already thinking about your circumstances. It also lets them know you're actively engaged in thinking about possible outcomes and solutions before you came to them. This is a great engagement strategy.

Never wing it. Be as specific and deliberate as possible. Always be prepared in advance. Make sure to write your questions down and have an idea where you want the conversation to go. Your commitment to being prepared shows them you are serious about investing in these relationships. It also shows them you are committed to respecting their time and you are looking for specific feedback—not general ideas.

These steps help you build the relationship to a point where they'll want to continue to connect and share with you. They move quickly to a point where they want to invest back into you and contribute to your development. The more open you are as you engage with your mentors, the more they will want to invest personally with you.

Imagine if you were to dump out all your problems and say, "How do I fix them?" While some people could handle that question, your board members may feel more used than valued with this approach.

Remember you are not looking for someone to solve your problems for you. You are looking to expand your perspective through the wisdom, insight, and experience of others so you can make quality decisions for your life, both personally and professionally.

Investing in right relationships and engaging meaningfully with your board members starts by sharing the framework of your situation. You do that by being specific and strategic. Show them you have thought about it and you have an initial idea about a plan. From there, share bite-size pieces. Ask questions focused

on the issue at hand and not the whole scenario. You
may think sharing the whole context is important but
allowing your board to ask for more details is the better approach. This will better position them to ask
probing questions and gather more information. They
can then give you their ideas or suggestions on which
direction to take, or they can offer questions or ideas
to investigate based on their experience. You will also
be able to gauge if a prospective board member is too
eager to offer advice.

In his book *Convertible Referrals,* Shaun Irwin
provides insight into the importance of investing well
in the right relationships. He addresses how to engage
others with intent:

"Don't plan to waste their time but if you're prepared
to listen well, learn, and execute on advice, I believe
you'll find more than enough mentors to help you gain
purchase in your given field and beyond.

"Be prepared to be challenged. All progress starts
with the truth. Do you have a plan for success that you
can share with these great minds? What are the specific
questions you want to ask each one in your interview
process? … Most important: Do you intend to listen
and execute or are you solely soliciting the magic bullet?

"Be ready to be held accountable. Busy, successful
people want to help and inspire others; they don't want
to waste time repeatedly going over the same things.
Listen well, take notes, be prepared to make commitments and then execute. If it doesn't work, you'll have
far more to discuss than if you didn't get to it at all or
went at it half-baked."[2]

That advice is golden! Resolve in your mind to
make the investment a win-win for both parties. Your

commitment to being prepared and then following through with any action items discussed and agreed upon is one of the best ways to honor the relationship you are building.

Feed the desire in others to invest in your development and you will gain an invaluable depth in your relationships. This strategy will also help you develop leadership skills that will allow you to grow in your own ability to lead others now and in the future.

▲

Trust

In his book *The Trust Edge*, David Horsager provides a definition of trust. He says, "Trust is the confident belief in someone or something. It is the confident belief in an entity: to do what is right, to deliver what is promised, to be the same every time, whatever the circumstances. Trust implies being reliable, dependable, and capable."[3]

Investing in someone or something means being intentional about how you spend your time, talent, and emotional energy. It takes a specific effort to develop an understanding of one another to gain the trust and confidence so you can be free to open up over time.

Trust is a reliance on the integrity, strength, ability, and surety of another person. Trust is about confidence in that other person. It is earned and not assumed. Trust is built over time and is one of the benefits of investing in relationships with others.

Building a trust relationship is the cornerstone of a strong mentor/mentee bond. The value you receive is enhanced by the level of trust you develop with members of your board. Trust most often manifests itself in the following ways: confidence, privacy, asking questions, opening up, being transparent, being vulnerable, and seeking forgiveness, gratitude, friendship, and encouragement.

As you look at strengthening many areas of your life, your personal board should also reflect a variety of experiences.

For example, you may want key partners in business who can guide you through a job transition, interview, promotion, or career development. In your personal life, you may want to connect with someone with more experience who can instruct and guide you in strengthening your marriage or raising your children. In your spiritual journey, you may want to connect with a leader from your place of worship or someone who lives out their faith and can lead you in a study or plan for personal spiritual growth.

Remember as you invite people in, you will uncover perspectives that can help you grow and develop in all areas of your life. These experiences allow you to go deeper and grow in ways you could never experience on your own.

▲

Lifelong Relationships

The ultimate benefit of properly investing in right relationships is the development of lifelong friendships. The idea is to move beyond the point of considering each other to be business associates or committee members. Take the time to get to know someone on a personal level and you will reap the great rewards of building a lifelong connection.

When I was let go from my position in 2012, I was disappointed to think of the clients I would not see regularly. I remember discussing my job change situation with Matt, one of my long-standing clients. I had helped him grow his business through our product line, and in the process, I learned about his life, marriage, motivations, and dreams. When we discussed being unsure of whether or not we would have the opportunity to continue working together, he said to me, "Z-Man, our relationship went beyond work a long time ago. This will not stop us from getting together and staying connected."

I was grateful to hear his response and valued the fact that we had been building a friendship throughout our years working together.

Building lasting relationships starts with listening and learning about the other person. Commit to learn about their life circumstances, and regularly ask about the things that are important to them in work and in life.

I find time and again when I feel comfortable enough to share about my own challenges, it opens doors to discuss life issues for both of us.

▲

Long-Term Strategy

Each relationship you develop is built around the idea of connecting for the long-term benefit of both parties. Don't settle for a popcorn approach where someone pops into your life for a brief moment and then disappears.

It's not about whatever pops into your head at a given time. It's about a long-term strategy for development and growth.

The investment you make in building the relationships with your board members is designed to expand your own thinking and help you grow as you develop your leadership muscles. Once I embraced the importance of building these relationships, it became a lifelong growth goal for me to continue to expand my thinking. Growing to your full potential does not happen by sitting in isolation. It happens by connecting with those who have gone before you, especially those who are willing to share and encourage you in your personal growth.

▲

"Personal relationships are the fertile soil from which all advancement, all success, all achievement in real life grows."

--*Ben Stein*--

CHAPTER 6
Highlights

- Investing in right relationships is your responsibility.

- How you want to engage and connect is up to you. This is your Board of Directors. You decide how you'll connect.

- You determine which areas you want guidance for: personal, professional, spiritual, etc.

- Whenever you face a significant decision in your life, you should reach out for a minimum of two perspectives. One is not enough!

- You get to decide what is significant for you.

- When you invest in building relationships, both parties will prosper.

- Always be prepared before engaging a member of your board. Never wing it. Be as specific and deliberate as possible.

- "Busy, successful people want to help and inspire others; they don't want to waste time repeatedly going over the same things. Listen well, take notes, be prepared to make commitments and then execute."

- Trust is a reliance on the integrity, strength, ability, and surety of another person.

- Trust is built over time and is one of the benefits of investing in relationships with others.

- Building a trust relationship is the cornerstone of a strong mentor/mentee bond.

CHAPTER 7
MAKE THE CALL

"It is not always what we know or analyzed before we make a decision that makes it a great decision. It is what we do after we make the decision to implement and execute it that makes it a good decision."

--William Pollard--

After spending time making connections and doing some initial investigation as to whether someone qualifies to be on your personal Board of Directors, you must make the move to decision time. You've done your homework. You've conducted interviews and considered leadership qualities of those who you've spoken with in order to see if they quality in helping you expand your perspective and grow your thinking.

After looking at the key strategies you want and need from these relationships, it's time to make the call by giving a formal invitation to those you want on your personal Board of Directors.

There are four key elements that drive the decision and should be consistent for all of your board members. They should all agree to:

1. Listen

2. Ask clarifying questions

3. Give honest feedback

4. Provide guidance or direction/suggestions

Remember, you are not looking for someone to come in and solve your problems. You are looking for those who will open your perspective to a level greater than you can achieve on your own. You're looking for people who will help expand your thinking so you can make quality decisions for your life both personally and professionally.

Here is a closer look at the key factors you should consider in determining who sits on your personal board. Spend some time looking for people who will bring the following qualities to a mentoring relationship:

1. **Listening.** You want someone willing to listen to you as you share your circumstances and your questions. If they rush to solve your problems, they may not be right for your board. If they are quick to interrupt you as you share, they may not be right for you. Listening is a key skill and a sign of a good leader.

2. **Clarifying questions.** You want someone who seeks to understand your circumstances by asking for additional information through clarifying questions.

Examples:

Tell me more about how you arrived at this juncture?
What has led you to that conclusion?
In addition, is there anything else I need to know about this issue?
What was your initial reaction to what happened?
Where do you want to go from here?

The best decisions come from the best and most complete information. A former boss, Rick Larson (not the one who let me go), taught me two specific lessons about decision-making that have stuck with me for nearly 20 years:

- Sometimes you have to go all the way around the bases before you can make a decision—meaning it's important to gather all the information necessary to evaluate the circumstances before making a decision.

- Don't make decisions in the heat of the battle. The closer you are to a challenge (from a timing and emotional perspective), the more likely you are to over-react in your decision. Decisions made in the heat of the moment are seldom in line with the correct long-term strategy you ultimately want to achieve. Take the time to settle down emotionally and focus on the facts as you "go around the bases" before deciding. You want someone who is willing to ask questions, not have all the answers!

Finding board members who are skilled at asking clarifying questions will help you become a better decision-maker.

3. **Honest feedback.** You don't want someone who will always agree with you. You want someone who is willing to be honest in how they see your situation and how you would or would not fit into it. This perspective is critical to your development.

Be willing to receive the perspective of others who know you and can honestly communicate to you what they see and know through their own experience. Allow them to use their own lens to view your talents, skills, and abilities. Keep yourself open to hearing the honesty of others.

4. **Direction.** You are looking for suggestions to consider or information to gather to help you make better decisions. Direction is about a suggestion or idea to consider. It's not about telling you what you should do! The next steps are always an important part of the process in mentoring. Make sure you leave a meeting or conversation with a plan to circle back, providing feedback or results. This idea of closing the loop adds value to your mentors and confirms and deepens your relationship. It also confirms and strengthens their credibility with you.

▲

The Invitation

Now that you've made the decision to stop going it alone by creating a new mindset, looking for influence in others, and then beginning the process of investing in those relationships you feel right about, it's time to formalize it. It's time to make specific invitations to those you want to join you on your journey. Opening the door of your heart to others is a point of significant growth you should not take for granted. This is where you take the next step on your path to the top and put all your work into action.

When you're confident you have identified people who will listen, ask clarifying questions, give honest feedback, and provide direction, you're ready to start inviting people to join your Board of Directors. It's time to make the call.

Here's how that conversation might sound:

"I am interested in building a team of mentors, a personal Board of Directors. I would like to invite you to be on my board. Before you answer, I want you to know what I'm looking for. I want someone who is willing to listen to the challenges and opportunities that come up in my life, ask good questions, provide honest feedback, and then share from your experience any wisdom and insight that will help guide me to making quality decisions. I'm not looking for you to solve my problems. I am looking to expand my perspective and would value your influence, leadership, and insight in helping me see any blind spots in my thinking or confirm I am on track. Any suggestions about anyone else I should talk to would also be greatly appreciated. I will not waste your time or ask you to commit to a regular meeting schedule. Let me know if you have any questions before you decide. Thanks for considering this request."

Or

If that seems too formal for you and the person you want to invite, here's a more casual version:

"I would like you to consider allowing me to reach out to you periodically either on a semi-regular basis or when I have a situation come up. I would like to be able to bounce my circumstances by you to get your perspective on options for handling what comes up in my life. My only request is you listen to my circumstances, be willing to ask any questions you have, and be honest with me in your feedback before sharing your suggestions."

Or

It may be as simple as this. You ask them to mentor you. You say, "Would you be willing to mentor me? I am looking for someone I could connect with periodically or when a challenge or opportunity comes up in my life. I will not bring my problems to you and ask you to solve them for me, but I am looking for your assistance by listening, asking questions, providing honest feedback, and sharing any suggestions you have to help me clarify my thinking."

No matter how you ask you must be clear on what it is you are looking for in a mentor. Be straightforward in the initial request and then be specific in your next step. Say to them, "Here's what I'm looking for. When we get together to discuss an issue I'm facing, my expectations from you would be the following: I want you to be willing to listen to my issues/opportunities and ask clarifying questions to make sure we are on the same page. The most important thing I could ask of you is to give me your honest feedback, no matter what it is, and help me think of next steps or questions to ask or other people to consider talking to. Can I count on you to do that for me?"

"Before you answer me, I want you to know what my commitment to you will be. I won't come and dump my life in front of you and say, 'fix this for me.' It will be my responsibility to engage with you periodically. There may be a season in life where I am going to need to talk to you more regularly. There may also be a time where I may not need to talk to you about my issues for an extended period."

"I'm not asking you to put me on your calendar every month where you have to fit me in and have lunch or coffee. I am open to doing that for a particular issue or a season of life but I'm not asking for that level of commitment from you. I am only asking you to be available when I feel the need arise to discuss items or issues in my life when I want to make sure my thinking is lined up with where I want to go."

When you've selected your board members and begin meeting, you'll seek to learn from their influence, input, experience, wisdom, and insight. When you meet, you want to lay out the groundwork for your circumstances and ask specific questions to invite them to engage through listening and asking clarifying questions of *you*. This process is an important part of every meeting. Don't skimp here. Make sure they are fully briefed on your circumstances to ensure the feedback they give you will assist in your decision making.

▲

The Relationship

You are not looking for someone to join your board based upon their schedule. You want someone to join you based upon their heart. Are you someone they would want to engage with when the need arises?

There are times when I will meet and open up to my mentors and then they will open up to me with some of their own issues. They are comfortable doing so because we have built a relationship of openness, honesty, and transparency where they feel like they can discuss most anything. We have a trust relationship, and we keep all issues discussed in confidence—just between us.

My relationship choices are built around helping me expand my perspective and climb to new heights personally and professionally. I move forward from first understanding I can't go it alone, and then I have the privilege to decide who joins me in the journey.

I can tell you firsthand through building my own board I have grown in ways I never could have achieved all by myself.

I have learned I couldn't reach those new heights when I was lost in my own thinking. It was only through the wisdom, insight, and experience of those who I learned to trust that I could expand my perspective and see beyond my own capabilities.

▲

The Power of Perspective

Back in 2012 when I lost my job, I found myself talking with members of my personal Board of Directors almost daily. Within the first two weeks of being laid off I met with a business owner who asked what he could do to help me. He suggested I consider going to work for him to train his young sales team and help them succeed in the same way I had helped him and his staff grow their business over the previous eight years. I told him I needed to think about it since I didn't have a fully written sales training program and would need to develop one.

This offer caused me to start thinking about building and developing a training curriculum. As I thought about turning away from sales and building a sales training program, I met with Dave, one of my board members. He asked me to walk him through my thinking, and I described this meeting and the opportunity before me. I continued talking about making a shift from what I had been doing to now developing an education and training program. I didn't feel I could accept this offer without having something in place, so I was ready to stop what I was doing and start down this path of training and development.

Dave then gave me one of the most important pieces of advice I have ever received. He said, "Jim, I know what you are thinking. I want you to consider another perspective. Most people in your situation start thinking about what they don't have and turn their backs on what they are good at to pursue something they are missing. When you get caught up in deficit thinking, you often take your eyes off your strengths and focus on your areas of weakness. I would ask you to consider another approach. Don't let your mortgage become your boss."

I asked him what he meant by that, and he went on to encourage me to find a job that lined up with my strengths right now, so I would make sure to take care of my family first. He told me in finding a job that pays me for the value I can bring to the table right away, it would give me the freedom to pursue other areas knowing my family was taken care of. He suggested if I turn away from what I'm good at and start pursuing something that doesn't pay me right away, I put myself in a position where I could eventually be controlled by the pressure of making my mortgage payment. If I go that route, the pressure will continue to mount. Dave finished by saying, "Take care of your family first, and once you find a job you can do well, start to lay out a plan to develop areas where you are not currently ready to launch."

Suddenly, I had a clearer vision of what to do. I thanked Dave for his advice, and as I reflected on his suggestion, it seemed to make perfect sense. I was caught up in viewing what I didn't have and was ready to put energy into writing and developing without bringing any money in to the household. I confirmed this suggestion and received affirmation from two additional board members. This perspective gave me the vision to take care of my family first by finding a job I could excel at right away. Once I started pursuing this path, I found a job within the next four weeks which provided work that lined up within my skill set—and at an increase in pay over my previous job.

I then set goals for writing and other pursuits outside of my daily work knowing I was taking care of my family first. This gave me an amazing sense of freedom and took away the serious pressure that comes from being controlled by my expenses.

Years later, I find myself still working in my area of strength and I'm pursuing writing, speaking, and training as a long-term strategy.

Don't be surprised when other leaders want to give back and share their ideas and experiences with you. Embrace it and engage with the people who you feel will bring the right areas of influence into your life. Be open and honest enough with yourself to listen to their insight. Remember, your growth is magnified when you engage with people who have gone ahead of you.

The wisdom, insight, and experience of others can help you see things from a different perspective and potentially open your eyes to see the entire picture of your circumstances.

▲

Your Team

This is it. This is your time. This is where you stand at the threshold of a decision. If you haven't already done so, it's time for you to step across the line and make the call as to who you will invite to be on your personal Board of Directors. Now is the time to trust it and move ahead with your decision to invite people to participate with you on your journey.

Everyone should have a minimum of three to five people on their personal board. Fewer than three limits your view and may not provide a broad enough range of experience or insight. You can certainly have more than five, but don't shoot for a twelve-member board! Remember, this is not a corporate structure. You want to be able to manage it. Building your personal Board of Directors is a process. It will typically be built up one at a time as you grow your board up to three to five people where you will receive plenty of great experience to expand your perspective.

Once you have invited your team to join you, you are on your way to the top. You'll experience a new and exciting level of confidence about what you're doing and where you're going!

When I was ready to raise the bar on my commitment to writing, I registered for a writing conference. The day before I left Minnesota for the conference, I reached out to all five members of my personal Board of Directors. By the time I had landed after the first leg of my trip and was waiting to board the second flight, I had heard back from all five members, four by text and one phone call. They all had responded to my request for feedback, guidance, prayer, and wisdom as I went to this conference for the first time. I was so blessed by their encouragement I went into the conference filled with confidence knowing my team was with me! When I got back from the weekend, they all wanted to hear how it went. I was able to share my experiences and thank each of them for their support and encouragement.

Build your team and see the vision of your future with a peak perspective!

▲

"A wise man makes his own decisions, an ignorant man follows the public opinion."

--Grantland Rice--

CHAPTER 7
Highlights

- After looking at the key strategies you want and need from these relationships, it's time to make the call.

- The four key elements of participation for your board members are:

  o Listen

  o Ask clarifying questions

  o Give honest feedback

  o Provide guidance or direction/suggestions

- Remember you are not looking for someone to come in and solve your problems.

- This is about expanding your perspective so you can make quality decisions for your life, both personally and professionally.

- You are not looking for someone to join your board based upon their schedule. You are looking for someone to join you based upon their heart.

- You won't grow to new heights when you're lost in your own thinking.

- Don't be surprised when other leaders want to give back and share their ideas and experience with you.

- This is where you stand at the threshold of a decision. It's time for you to step across the line and make the

call as to who you will invite to be on your personal
Board of Directors.

- You should have a minimum of three to five people
  on your personal board.

- Build your team and see the vision of your future
  with a peak perspective.

CHAPTER 8

BE THE DIFFERENCE

"The man on top of the mountain didn't fall there."

--Vince Lombardi--

Growing up, I often heard a forward-thinking encouragement from my parents, "You can be anything you want to be." Well, with eight siblings, sometimes that simply meant I wanted to *be* alone, or just *be* myself. When I was younger I dreamed of *being* a professional baseball player or *being* a professional golfer.

I dreamed of being the one ... to drive in the winning run ... to hit the clutch shot ... to make the difference for the team.

It didn't take long for reality to set in. I played baseball for seven years and only dabbled in golf when I was younger. Once I got to college, I needed to work to pay my tuition. During school I was working 26 hours a week at a restaurant, and for five summers in a row

I also worked for my dad's building supply company. That was five summers of working two jobs, seven days a week! I wasn't afraid to work hard, motivated to finish college debt-free. That left little time for anything else during my college years. I played softball a couple of nights a week to keep active. I enjoyed the creative side of business and focused in on a marketing degree from the University of St. Thomas, in Saint Paul, Minnesota. As the first sibling with a degree in my family, I was excited about what I had accomplished, yet I still had little idea of what I really wanted to do with my life.

After graduation and a job search, I sat down with my dad and he discussed the idea of moving from driving a truck and working in the warehouse to working in the office for his business. This became the real-life training ground for me and taught me in new ways about being in a people business.

As I grew in my career, I developed a greater desire to connect with and learn from other people. This didn't happen overnight. It took years of experience and many mistakes to realize the best way to make a lasting connection with others was not only to take but also to give back to them in ways that left a positive impact. I would work to help, encourage, and lead others to excellence in their lives—a passion that continued to develop in me through my career in sales and as a corporate trainer for a professional education company.

▲

Perspective

There's a big difference in perspective between look-ing up at a mountain and looking down at a mountain range. When looking up, you can easily get caught up in the size and scope of the mountain in front of you with little to no understanding that there is so much more to see beyond the mountain. We get so focused on what's in front of us our perspective remains limited to only what we can see.

But here's what I've discovered: You can't see what you can't see!

Once you reach the top and can see over the moun-tain, you'll realize there is still much more to see. More mountains, fields, and valleys. When you arrive at the top of the mountain with the help of your personal board, you'll become keenly aware of two things: the new perspective you have with your expanded view and the path you took to get there.

▲

See Value in a New Way

When confronted with new vistas, it's easy to be over-whelmed, especially if you think you have to start navigating solo from here. The effectiveness of your next move depends on your ability to connect with your board. Remember, you can climb to the top by yourself, but that doesn't make you a leader.

Having a personal Board of Directors allows you to see with greater clarity. When you climb to the top with guidance from your team of mentors, you have a better understanding of the process—and the value of not going it alone. You now know and understand the benefit of having your perspective expanded, and you will eventually become compelled to do the same for others.

Your experience will make you more visible to others around you who will want to know what you've been doing. This shift is partly due to you becoming less self-centered and more willing to share and be a team player. You will start to get noticed for all the right reasons.

Your personal Board of Directors can help you find your heartbeat to know why you are here and what you are meant to do. This is an exciting time in your life. Your purpose becomes clearer, and you feel alive in what you do. This is when you start to make quality decisions about where you are going next.

As you face the circumstances of work and life and gather advice and feedback from your personal board, you will grow personally and enhance your ability to read and respond to similar circumstances in the future. You will strengthen your capacity and position yourself to be available as a mentor for someone else's personal Board of Directors.

As you invest in others, you may be amazed at how often you find yourself being invited to coffee to connect with someone who is looking for a mentor in their life. This is one of the great joys of giving back and sowing into others in the same way you have benefited from the mentorship of others in your own life.

Part of the great value in your personal development is finding your own sweet-spot—what you're good at and how you are wired. It's different for everyone and can be very rewarding once you realize where your strengths lie.

Having you own team of mentors to engage with you and get to know you will help you recognize what you're good at and guide you to make decisions that line up with your strengths.

▲

Open Heart, Open Mind

Have you ever walked into a situation—a conference, a meeting, or a party—uncertain of what was going to happen or why you were there, only to find you were surprised and uplifted by the experience?

Some of your greatest experiences will come to you when you have an open heart and an open mind. Your willingness to entertain new ideas and new possibilities for your future direction is just the beginning. Real growth comes when you allow those on your board to help you recognize the opportunities and pitfalls before you. When you are willing to be open and share your ideas, assumptions, challenges, and fears, you will grow leaps and bounds over going it alone. Your openness, in turn, becomes the heartbeat of your ability to be the difference for someone else.

This experience allows you to see the future state of mentoring as you transition to serving in the same capacity for others.

▲

Grow

Submitting myself to the wisdom, insight, and experience of others brought me to a place of new perspectives. It also gave me the gift of a positive attitude. I became more confident and encouraged as I expanded my perspective and found my positivity became contagious. I became hungry for more information and pursued all the books and resources I could find on leadership and communication. I became hungry to learn and apply these truths about effectively dealing with, leading, and adding value to the lives of others. If I could narrow it down to one key perspective it would be this:

Adding value to other people became my heartbeat.

▲

Receive, Strengthen, and Sow

When I became open to others and was willing to humble myself and become a student, I found it easier to accept and incorporate the wisdom and insight others were willing to share with me. This gave me strength and clarity as I grew personally and began making better decisions. This also opened my heart up with a desire to give to others in the same way my board had given to me.

You'll find your transition from being the receiver of value to being the difference for others is built on three ideas: receive, strengthen, and sow.

Receive

- Open your heart to the wisdom, insight and experience of others
- Gather input that allows you to make quality decisions

Humility and trust are the foundational elements which help you receive from those who want the best for you. The more transparent and honest you are, the greater the impact will be on the value of connecting with others you trust.

Your willingness to receive from others helps you make the best decisions for your personal and professional life.

Strengthen

- Expand your capacity to think through challenges and opportunities
- Engage your board regularly to keep growing

With each opportunity to connect with members of your board, you will expand your perspective and increase your capacity to navigate similar circumstances in the future, not only for you, but also for others who may seek your advice.

As you keep regular contact with your board, you will increase your understanding and develop a level of discernment that allows you to continue to grow.

Sow

- Give back by sharing with others the same benefits you have received
- Leave a legacy of adding value to others

Just as your personal Board of Directors has sown value into your life, you'll want to be ready and willing to share with others. Giving back is its own rich reward. You may be surprised how many people don't have any mentors in their life to turn to. Maybe you can be the difference by giving back in the same manner you've received—the impact can be life-changing.

Where most people fail is when they choose not to do anything with what they've been given, even the shared wisdom and experience of others. Don't be that person. Make a decision to pass on what you've learned and sow into the lives of others.

▲

Moving Ahead

"When the student is ready the teacher will appear."[1] This is an old Buddhist proverb which speaks to the first step in moving ahead—being ready. When you make the decision to grow, you will put yourself in position to receive from others—teachers, coaches, counselors, mentors, leaders, etc. This is where you will learn from the counsel and advice of others who've gone before you. As a student, you should strive to embrace humility as your posture to keep you from blocking the information being shared with you, being open to the wisdom, insight, and experience of others as they share with you.

Have you ever attended an event where, even though there was a large crowd, it seemed as if the speaker was speaking directly to you? It was as if someone had fed the speaker your specific life circumstances. This is an example of the *student* being ready to hear what the *teacher* has to say. This is not a coincidence. It's real. It is you learning you are not alone in how you feel or in what you are going through.

Are you the student, ready to put into practice this teaching about developing your personal Board of Directors with the goal of eventually being a mentor to others? The proof is in what you do next.

You've come to the point where you have had others join your personal Board of Directors and share with you from their own experience. You have put yourself in a position to learn and grow from their wisdom and insight. You've allowed them to add value to your life as you have reaped the benefit of what they have sown into you. Now it's time for you to go and sow into the lives of others. Be ready to join them in their journey and lead them up their mountain.

▲

"The successful attainment of a dream is a cart and horse affair. Without a team of horses, a cart full of dreams can go nowhere."

--*Rex Murphy*--

CHAPTER 8
Highlights

- You can't see what you can't see.

- When you climb to the top with guidance from your team of mentors, you have a better understanding of the process and the value of not going it alone.

- Some of your greatest experiences will come to you when you have an open heart and an open mind.

- Submitting yourself to the wisdom, insight, and experience of others will bring you to a place of new perspectives.

- The greatest impact in being the difference for others is built on the following three ideas: receive, strengthen, and sow.

- Make a decision to pass on what you've learned and sow into the lives of others.

- Join others in their journey and lead them up their mountain.

PART THREE

HIGHER VIEW

LEAD ON

CHAPTER 9

GROW AS A LEADER

Leadership doesn't come from headlines or spot-lights. It's the influence that's formed in your daily decisions.

One thing that stands out to me in my years of reading, listening, engaging, watching, and conversing with leaders is they are always working on growing. Some would say leaders don't stop; they go. I like to think of it this way: *Leaders don't arrive, they grow.*

I've never known a true leader who stops reading, gathering information, listening to others, or stops learning. I remember in my early development in understanding leadership, I heard the following sayings:

"Leaders are readers."

"Leaders listen. They don't do all the talking."

"We all have the same 24 hours in a day. This difference between you and industry leaders is the books they read, the people they associate with, and the way they spend their time."

I heard these words as a call to action.

To put this in perspective: Once I got my degree in marketing, I set books aside for a while and spent any "reading" time with Sports Illustrated, Golf Digest, Golf magazine, and the sports page of the local newspaper. At that point in my young life, I didn't feel the need to read any more books—especially those that felt like textbooks from school.

When challenged by the phrase "leaders are readers," I became curious about how to change my ways. I started by setting aside time to read for 15 minutes at the end of each day. This may not seem like a lot, but committing to reading by putting positive thoughts and bigger picture ideas in my head started me down the path of making a habit of reading every day. I started reading books on leadership and learning how to work well and get along with others. One of the first books that had a big impact on me was *How to Win Friends and Influence People* by Dale Carnegie. This jolted me to a new place of impact and taught me how to relate to people as I learned about myself.

Reading has now become so ingrained in me I can't go a day without reading, and I typically have two books going at the same time, one in the morning and one in the evening. I've become and remain hungry to keep learning.

Daily habits make a difference in the development of our leadership qualities. I've learned to put simple tasks into action to form daily habits which have had a lasting effect on my ability to lead.

Do you want to be a more effective leader? Be honest with yourself about your own schedule and then make the necessary adjustments to move toward what you want. Your daily habits will set you on a course to keep growing in your leadership one step at a time. Be consistent. What you do daily will make all the difference down the road. Leadership doesn't come from headlines or spotlights. It's the influence that's formed in your daily decisions.

The more you read about leadership and working well with others, the more you will find yourself growing in your career and set yourself up to be promoted or invited into leadership roles.

▲

Growth

A common misperception about growth is it happens as the result of building on one success after another. Growth is just as much the result of managing yourself through your failures. Growth comes with the determination to get up, regardless of your circumstances, and move ahead.

When considering where growth actually happens, consider the mountains and the valleys. Fruit doesn't typically grow at or near the top of the mountain. The greatest growth takes place in the valley and up the slope of the mountain. That's where the fertile soil is.

If you are struggling because your think you are at the bottom—down in the valley—be encouraged! You are surrounded by fertile soil. You can grow right where you are, step by step, until you reach the top of the mountain.

In his book *Integrity*, Dr. Henry Cloud talks about the importance of growing by submitting to others: "Another aspect of growth characteristics is the ability to seek out and submit to 'mentors,' or people who are further down the road. They can take input, and modeling, and are not ashamed to ask for it."

"When you interview successful people, they will always be able to go back and see the major growth seasons of their lives being launched and guided by mentors," Cloud says. "Some of these relationships were informal, and some more structured. But, virtually all people who leave good wakes have submitted themselves to the input of people, 'further down the road.' And, the interesting thing is they tend to do it for life, not just in the early years. They always value the experience of others and willingly take it in."[1]

Don't miss the key ideas in the last two statements. People who value having mentors in their lives don't stop after they have experienced growth. They are more likely to "do it for life" and "always value the experience of others." This is a true sign of someone interested in continuing on a growth plan.

▲

Leadership

There is a big difference between your desire to lead and your effectiveness in leading. By expanding your own perspective, you put yourself in a better position to add awareness and discernment in your leadership in a way you couldn't before.

One of my favorite stories about a leader who thinks he's arrived is from John Maxwell's book *Developing the Leader Within You*. Maxwell says, "My favorite leadership proverb is: He who thinketh he leadeth and hath no one following him is only taking a walk."[2] Priceless!

Don't let that be you. Leaders must earn buy-in from their team. Leaders send a different message than managers or bosses. They are constantly talking about what *we* will do, what *we* can accomplish, how *we* will get there, etc.

Manager vs. Leader:

MANAGER	LEADER
Demands respect	Earns respect
Enforces compliance	Invites collaboration
Focuses on procedures	Focuses on growth
Assigns blame for failure	Engages in problem-solving
Thinks about their position	Thinks about their people

▲

Open Your Eyes

Another way I learned about leadership was by becoming aware of what was going on around me. Leadership was always there; I just didn't always recognize it. Growing up, I saw how my dad and mom led the family. They were both actively involved in our development and always encouraged us to go and do and be our best. Sometimes, leadership is being silent amid chaos, or being steady in the storms of life, or setting the pace when no one wants to make a decision. I watched as my dad always had a sense of where he was going and what he wanted to do. He was a great leader that had special impact on each of his nine children. We were all different, and he was playful and calm with each of us. We could count on him to always be steady when our worlds were stormy. We could always count on him for his opinion and perspective, usually with a little gleam in his eye as he shared.

As I set out on my own I learned to observe others:

How did they handle tough situations?

What were the keys to navigating through uneasy circumstances?

How did they know?

Where did they turn?

In his book *Care to Dare*, George Kohlrieser shares the importance of having a secure base from which to develop and grow your leadership skills. Kohlrieser stresses how having your own "leadership lifeline" is a great measure of your own leadership storyline. He states, "Leadership is a culmination of life experiences and intentional development efforts. Secure Base Leaders recognize the power of their past and fully understand how the history of their beliefs, habits, and relationship patterns impacts their leadership." He emphasizes how leaders have learned from their past, both positive and negative. From those experiences, your leadership choices become a conscious decision for what you want as you move forward in life.

Another great tip Kohlrieser shares is, "Find another person and work on your Lifelines together. When you share the experience and confide in someone else, you enhance the learning experience …. the questions asked by the other person may prompt insights and 'a-ha' moments. Plus, you will learn about the other person and create an opportunity for a deeper bond."

Kohlrieser affirms the power of mentorship, noting, "You will not gain the same depth of experience or insight by simply doing this exercise alone."[3]

Remember, *Leaders don't arrive; they grow!* Keep a growth mindset alive throughout your life.

▲

Experience

Along the journey of writing this book, I have interviewed a number of people to find out their strategies to keep learning and growing. One friend likes to get his information and leadership training during his morning walk as he gets his "steps" in, accomplishing his daily step goal on his Fitbit while listening to audio books. He gets his headset on and gets moving, feeding his brain as he takes care of his body!

I asked another friend and business leader about his mentors. He named a few but also told me his greatest influence comes from his "University on Wheels." He has a long commute each day and listens to audio books or podcasts daily, both to and from work. This has kept him fresh and up to date on trends in leadership and in the marketplace. He is one of the smartest marketing minds I know, and he leads a team of people in his company who have always been loyal and fully committed to the company's mission.

Still others I interviewed spoke of their own commitment to reading for personal and professional development. This could very well be a call to you to set a goal in the New Year, or even the next quarter. Make plans to fill your mind with books, podcasts, webinars, etc., that can impact your personal and professional development. I don't know too many people who are strategic and intentional about personal development who didn't also increase their impact professionally in some capacity.

My interviews have also brought some surprises. One friend I reconnected with told me he didn't have any mentors in his life. He said that years ago, when he faced a big career decision, he didn't have anyone to turn to. He crossed his fingers and made a choice and then decided to make it work. He said he didn't know any better, nor did he understand how to engage someone else in the decision process.

Another friend told me when he was growing up, he had people around him telling him he couldn't do it or wasn't good enough. When it came time to decide about sports or school or career pursuits, he came out of his teen years with no one on his side. He was on his own to make decisions. We spoke about this recently and I could still see the sting of the feeling he had and how he learned to work through it when he was all alone at some critical junctures in his life.

Another guy I met for coffee—referred to me for career encouragement—shared how he didn't know who to talk to about his career direction. I asked if he had any mentors in his life, and he said, "No." Of course, I shared with him the value of having a team of mentors … a personal Board of Directors. He asked for additional details and I laid out a game plan for him to get started. He left with a plan to get started building his own team of mentors.

In our individualistic culture in the United States, I shouldn't be surprised to find there are many people who don't have any mentorship structure in their lives, but it's a fact, and it is stories like these that have motivated me to write this book. I have been personally blessed by the value in having my own personal Board of Directors and want others to enjoy that same value as they take on the challenges and opportunities of life.

▲

Make the Most of Your Investment

When you make the decision to grow for the rest of your life, you are making a decision that will impact generations. You've come to recognize you can't go it alone and truly lead others. Building your personal Board of Directors and engaging them will continue to strengthen and enhance your ability to pivot and add value to others.

Make it a habit to invest in other people. Live out a positive attitude with the best intentions toward others. When you do, you add words to the music of your life.

▲

"Leadership requires the courage to make decisions that will benefit the next generation."

--Alan Autry--

CHAPTER 9
Highlights

- Leaders don't arrive; they grow!

- A common misperception about growth is it happens as the result of building on one success after another.

- Growth is really the result of managing yourself through your failures.

- Growth comes when you are determined to get up regardless of your circumstances and move ahead.

- People who value having mentors in their lives don't stop after they have experienced growth.

- When you make the decision to grow for the rest of your life, you are making a decision that will impact generations.

- Make it a habit to invest in other people.

CHAPTER 10

GIVE BACK

"Life's most persistent and urgent question is, 'What are you doing for others?'"

--Martin Luther King Jr.--

Rewards come in all shapes and sizes. Each of us is motivated by different things, so there isn't a specific reward that fits absolutely everyone, but I have one suggestion that comes close. It's not something you receive or define. It's something you give. It turns out to be the gift that is defined by the recipient.

The reward I'm talking about is a form of giving back. It involves investing what you've learned back into the lives of others on their journey. I refer to it as:

Leading others to succeed.

You see, I would much rather develop other leaders rather than manage other people, even if it's my own family! Helping others develop into leaders is a high calling.

Now, you don't get to define their success. They define what success means to them. You simply work on leading and guiding them up their mountain to realize their own success. This is rewarding in a way that's hard to describe. It brings a level of personal fulfillment and satisfaction that becomes a strong motivator for you to continue the mission of giving back.

The whole idea of being a giver and not a taker was foreign to me at first. Growing up surrounded by eight siblings meant I became very possessive; this affected my leadership and I needed to learn how to help others get what they want. I had to make mistakes and learn about the other person's point of view. It took me many years to improve my ability to take my eyes off myself and put them on other people. My growth in this area became exponential after I climbed the mountain to develop my personal Board of Directors and truly plugged in to their wisdom.

Once I had gained the benefit of a "peak perspective," people started asking me for advice! That seemed strange to me at first, yet as I shared my experiences and learned to start asking questions instead of making assumptions, it was a turning point for my own development. I was a more effective leader and of greater service to others when I practiced these principles as I engaged with them:

No assumptions.

Ask questions.

Find out what they are thinking.

Look for common experiences.

Share what I did right and what I did wrong.

If they could learn from my mistakes, all the better for them!

If you walk around with a "what's in it for me" mentality, then it's hard to see the needs of others. That focus may be fine for a time or a circumstance, but it should not be a resting place for you. I never thought of myself as a teacher, yet I find myself teaching others every day by my actions and my words. It's found in what I do and don't do and in what I say and don't say. We are always teaching.

▲

Be Open

Over the years of having my own personal board, I have found myself being asked or invited to connect with someone who is going through a hard time or facing a new opportunity. I determined to remain open to be helpful to anyone who asked, whenever I could.

I have always enjoyed helping others process their thinking by asking questions and finding out as much as I can about their situation to learn and understand what's important to them. It's only from that position I can confidently offer suggestions for them to consider in their decision-making process. I try not to tell them what to do. My role is to listen, ask questions, give honest feedback, counsel, guide, teach and encourage—just as my board has done for me. I must earn the right to be able to fill that role in the lives of others.

▲

Share

It's true you can't give away that which you don't possess. Now that you have grown in your own development as a leader, you are able to share your experiences with others.

Once you have navigated through a challenge or opportunity with the help and guidance of your personal board, you are able to provide the very same gift to others. Your experience through trials gives you credibility and insight in how to guide someone else through similar circumstances.

Don't get caught up in where you are. Get caught up in what got you there! Let the fundamentals you've experienced in your life be your guide. When your circumstances allow you to have a platform to share with others, don't run ahead blindly telling others how great you are.

Instead, stop. Look around you. Be honest with yourself.

No one knows more about what you have gone through to get where you are than you. Review the fundamentals that have allowed you to progress through the high points and the tough parts of your journey. As you look back over your path up the mountain, you can use what you've learned as a guide for how you can give back to others. The key characteristics of your mentors become the model you can use to be a mentor to others. Remember your purpose is not to tell them how you did it. It is to find out what they want and help guide them on their journey.

When setting expectations with those who request mentoring, recognize they may not know what to expect from you as a mentor. You can use the platform of listening, asking questions, giving honest feedback, and providing suggestions or direction as the road map to help you in mentoring with clear expectations for both parties.

Your experience becomes the foundation from which you will share the insight and wisdom you have learned along the way.

Remember this is not about give-to-get. This is a legacy move. *Just give.* When your heart pumps with a purpose to add value to the lives of other people, this becomes easier. It ends up being part of who you have become primarily as the result of others investing into your life. What a gift! Don't hoard it or keep it to yourself. Share it. Give it away and bless others.

▲

Legacy

The meaning of legacy exploded in my life to a level I could not have understood without experiencing the events of January 2013.

My father had been diagnosed with pancreatic cancer. No one could have imagined that in one week's time, after a normal family party on Sunday and then chemotherapy starting on Monday, he would be gone the following Sunday. It was the curveball we didn't see coming. Yes, we knew the cancer was serious, we just didn't know how far it had spread.

I was with my dad that Sunday afternoon. We shared many stories together that day. He told me, "One of the greatest blessings your mother and I have is knowing how all of you kids get along with each other." He was appropriately humble and proud of the legacy he built in raising his family. Not long after that, he collapsed, and I held him as he stopped breathing while we were waiting for the ambulance to arrive. It's hard to describe the physical feelings and the emotions of that experience. Each time I look back on that day, the word that keeps coming back to me again and again is legacy.

I think of the legacy he had been sowing into me from the beginning of my life—all the way up to that moment. Years later, I continue to reflect on how he loved me and my siblings and how he lived his life for others. He taught me the importance of family, friends, and faith, and never wavered in his focus in any of those areas. We are all better because of his leadership and his servant heart.

He taught me the importance of being a servant-leader. He showed me how to give back to others and take care of those in need. What a legacy. I only hope to live up to how he raised me—to live for, lead, and serve others.

▲

Dealing with Pain and Loss

What happens when a key mentor in your life is no longer there? What if a mentor's circumstances change or if they pass away, what will you do? How will you handle it? It can be a lonely feeling. It can leave you wondering where to turn. It can leave you with a gap in your life that may be hard to reconcile.

Such was the case for me when my father died. The gap I felt was more profound than I could have imagined. I wanted to call or visit him to discuss something that had come up only to find there was no one to answer the call. There was no opportunity to schedule me into his calendar. I ended up with a lonely feeling and spent a lot of time reflecting ...

What would dad say?

What questions would he ask?

What action would he take?

What has he shared in the past that might apply to my circumstances?

Although he wasn't the only mentor in my life, he was certainly the key influence in my growth and development. A great blessing, I have found from his impact on me is that his legacy continues to live on in my life.

Navigating loss takes on a new dimension in our thinking which often feels as though we are unprepared for our new circumstances. When loss happens, our response should be the same as we learned earlier about not going it alone.

This is not a time to isolate yourself. This is a time to act and engage your personal Board of Directors. Share your feelings and concerns. Be honest and transparent with them. You have some processing to do. Don't cut it short or keep it in. This will take some time, so give it all the time it needs. If in six months or a year after your loss you find yourself struggling emotionally about a new issue in your life and you wish you could bounce it off the person you've lost, don't beat yourself up and deny yourself the time to feel. Allow others to continue to walk along side of you, even your family and friends.

Also, don't be afraid to pursue professional counseling if you still struggle. Asking for help is not a sign of weakness. It is healthy for you to reach out in your time of need.

▲

Add Value

One of the most important discoveries for me as the result of having my own personal Board of Directors was learning the importance of adding value to other people. I have taught on this subject and shared with others about the benefits of having a personal board, but I didn't understand the depth of its value until I found myself in deep need as I faced various challenges and opportunities. My experiences along the way have taught me to freely share about the importance of having a team of mentors.

That is why I want you to know how valuable it is to surround yourself with people who have your best interests in mind, whether you are going through an uninvited challenge or a great opportunity.

I have loved the idea of adding value to others and consider it part of my heartbeat today. It's what really gets me excited about sharing experiences that can have a positive impact and lead others to greater heights in their own journey.

My hope is for you to discover your heartbeat along the way. When you learn what really motivates and excites you, you end up with more energy and ability to serve others. The things you have learned about yourself and learned from your personal Board of Directors will guide you to keep on moving, growing, leading, and giving.

When you expand your perspective, you can see, do, and understand things from a greater vantage point, and this allows you to share value and impact with others. Become the leader you were meant to be by sharing the benefits of having a peak perspective!

▲

Putting it All Together

Looking back over the connection between mentorship and leadership, five words help put it all together—Go, Climb, Grow, Lead, Give.

In the first section of this book, PART ONE: CHALLENGE – ALL ALONE, you explored the idea of not going it alone any more. It's here you discovered the importance of changing your strategy from doing things by yourself to beginning to engage others to help guide you through the challenges and opportunities of life. This is the starting point of your journey from where you are—right now! It's time to act—**Go**.

In the middle section, PART TWO: SOLUTION – DEVELOP YOUR PERSONAL BOARD OF DIRECTORS, you looked at the five steps as a guide to put together your own team of mentors—your personal Board of Directors. It's here you learned to customize a plan by you and for you, to climb to new heights and grow as a person and as a leader—**Climb/Grow**.

The last section, PART THREE: HIGHER VIEW – LEAD ON, found you standing on higher ground with a newly found peak perspective. From here you learned the importance of leading with impact, and influence that adds value to others and is not self-serving. It is also here that you learned the value of giving back and being available to help others climb their mountains—**Lead/Give.**

When your heart is filled with the value of having your own personal Board of Directors to help you make quality decisions for your personal and professional life, a natural by-product is your own desire to give the same gift you've received to others. You'll want to share it.

That's where my heart is, and it's what I wish for you—that you would begin your journey today and grow into a leader who ultimately makes a difference in the lives of those around you.

Become the leader you were meant to be!
Go. Climb. Grow. Lead. Give.

▲

"Find your voice and inspire others to find theirs."

--Stephen R. Covey--

CHAPTER 10
Highlights

- Lead others to succeed.

- Now that you have grown in your own development as a leader, you are able to share your experience with others.

- Once you have navigated through a challenge with the help and guidance of your personal board, you are now able to provide the very same gift to others.

- Don't get caught up in where you are. Get caught up in what got you there!

- Remember this is not about give-to-get. This is a legacy move. Just give.

- The things you have learned about yourself and learned from your personal Board of Directors will guide you to keep on moving, growing, leading, and giving.

- Go. Climb. Grow. Lead. Give.

ACKNOWLEDGEMENTS

To my wife, Nancy, who has blessed me in so many ways. Thank you for believing in me and for your love, support, insight, encouragement, and assistance in helping me refine the message of this book to turn it into a reality.

The inspiration for this book has come from the great men in my life who have had lasting impact on my personal and professional development.

To my father, Eugene Zugschwert, who set an example of emphasizing what it means to be committed to adding value to other people. He taught me that life is a people business and he showed me how to work well and get along with others by the way he lived out his legacy every day of his life.

To Dave Schaefer, John Zugschwert, Ken Clarke, Mark Kraemer, and Andy Garner. You have been more important to my personal growth and development than I could ever express. You have brought your honesty, integrity, experience, wisdom, insight, and perspective to our relationship. You are invaluable to me as mentors and guides as I navigate my way to new heights and I am forever grateful to each of you.

To Kary Oberbrunner, David Branderhorst, and the team at Author Academy Elite for your wisdom and guidance in helping me make this book a reality. To Nanette O'Neal, for her editing and encouragement. To LilaM, for her patience and skill in creating the cover design.

NOTES

Opening Quote: Woodrow Wilson, *http://www.brainyquote.com*, (Brainy Quote, BrainyMedia, Inc.)

INTRODUCTION

1. Robert Lewis, *Men's Fraternity – The Great Adventure, Session 3*, (Nashville, TN: Lifeway Press, 2006)

2. Alex and Stephen Kendrick, *Facing the Giants*, (IDP Studio, 2006) DVD

CHAPTER 1

Opening Quote: George Washington Carver, *http://www.brainyquote.com*, (Brainy Quote, BrainyMedia, Inc., 2017)

1. John C. Maxwell, *Thinking for a Change*, (Warner Business Books, 2003), 12.

2. Lt. Col. Rob "Waldo" Waldman, *Never Fly Solo*, (McGraw-Hill, 2010), Introduction: xvii.

3. Jack Nicklaus, *Jack Nicklaus' Playing Lessons*, (Golf Digest/Tennis, Inc., Turnbull, CT, 1976, 1977, 1978, 1979, 1980, and 1981, by Golden Bear, Inc.), 21.

4. John Boyette, *http://www.augusta.com, Jack Nicklaus-1965* (Augusta.com, Feb.17, 2012)

5. Andrew Sobel and Jerold Panas, *Power Questions*, (John Wiley & Sons, Hoboken, NJ, 2012), 4.

Closing Quote: Albert Einstein, *http://www.goodreads.com*, (Goodreads, Inc., 2018)

CHAPTER 2

Opening Quote: Carl Sandburg, *Today Matters*, John C. Maxwell, (Center Street/Hachette Book Group USA, 2004)

1. Dictionary.com – Mentor, *http://www.dictionary.com*, (Dictionary.com, 2018)

2. Stu Weber, *Four Pillars of a Man's Heart*, (Multnomah Publishers, Inc., 1997), 186.

3. Dictionary.com – Mentee, *http://www.dictionary.com*, (Dictionary.com, 2018)

4. Dan Fogelberg, *High Country Snows*, (Full Moon, 1985 Sony Music Entertainment)

5. David Cottrell, *Monday Morning Leadership*, (CornerStone Leadership Institute, Dallas, TX, 2002), 12, 13.

6.   Paul Batz and Tim Schmidt, *What Really Works*, (Beaver's Pond Press, Inc., Edina, MN, 2011), Introduction: xi, xii.

Closing Quote: John C. Maxwell, *Today Matters*, (Center Street/Hachette Book Group USA, 2004)

CHAPTER 3

Opening Quote: Kary Oberbrunner, *Day Job to Dream Job*, (Baker Books, 2014)

1.   Mark LeBlanc, *Never Be the Same*, (Expert Publishing, Inc, Andover, MN, 2010), 26.

Closing Quote: Earl Nightingale, *http://www.brainy-quote.com*, (Brainy Quote, BrainyMedia, Inc. 2017)

CHAPTER 4

Opening Quote: Andrew Carnegie, *http://www.goodreads.com*, (Goodreads, Inc., 2018)

1.   Jim Collins, *Good to Great*, (HarperCollins Publishers, Inc., 2001), 11.

2.   Simon Sinek, *Start With Why*, (Portfolio/Penguin, Penguin Group, 2009), 37, 38, 39.

3.   Richard J. Leider, *The Power of Purpose*, (Berrett-Koehler Publishers, Inc., 2015), 8.

4.   David Maraniss, *When Pride Still Mattered: A Life of Vince Lombardi*, (Simon & Schuster, Inc., 2000), 274.

5.   Ron Howard (Director), *Apollo 13*, (Universal Pictures, 1998)

6.   Dale Carnegie, *How to Win Friends and Influence People*, (Gallery Books, a division of Simon & Schuster, Inc., 1936), 129,130.

Closing Quote: Peter Diamandis, *http://www.brainy-quote.com*, (Brainy Quote, BrainyMedia, Inc., 2017)

CHAPTER 5

Opening Quote: President Woodrow Wilson, *http://www.brainyquote.com*, (Brainy Quote, BrainyMedia, Inc., 2017)

1.   John C. Maxwell, *The 21 Irrefutable Laws of Leadership*, (Thomas Nelson, 1998 and 2007), 11.

2.   Bob Burg and John David Mann, *The Go-Giver*, (Portfolio-The Penguin Group, 2007), 68.

Closing Quote: Stephen R. Covey, *http://www.brainyquote.com*, (Brainy Quote, BrainyMedia, Inc., 2017)

CHAPTER 6

Opening Quote: Clarence Francis, *http://www.inspiringquotes.us*, (Inspiring Quotes, 2016)

1.   Proverbs 27:17 – Holy Bible, New Living Translation, (Tyndale Charitable Trust, 1996), 681.

2.   Shaun Irwin, *Convertible Referrals*, (Convertible Referrals, 2013), 23, 24.

3. David Horsager, *The Trust Edge*, (Free Press, a division of Simon & Schuster, Inc., 2009), 8.

Closing Quote: Ben Stein, *http://www.brainyquote. com*, (Brainy Quote, BrainyMedia, Inc., 2018)

CHAPTER 7

Opening Quote: William Pollard, *http://www. brainyquote.com*, (Brainy Quote, BrainyMedia, Inc., 2017)

Closing Quote: Grantland Rice, *http://www.brainy-quote.com*, (Brainy Quote, BrainyMedia, Inc., 2017)

CHAPTER 8

Opening Quote: Vince Lombardi, *http://www.quote-fancy.com*, (Quotefancy, 2018)

1. Buddhist Proverb, *http://en.m.wikiversity.org*, (Wikiversity, Wikimedia Foundation, 2018)

Closing Quote: Rex Murphy, *Teamwork Makes the Dream Work*, John C. Maxwell (Thomas Nelson, Inc., 2002)

CHAPTER 9

Opening Quote: Jim Zugschwert

1. Dr. Henry Cloud, *Integrity*, (HarperCollins, 2006), 226.

2. John C. Maxwell, *Developing the Leader Within You*, (Thomas Nelson, Inc., 1993), 1.

3. George Kohlrieser, *Care to Dare*, (Jossey-Bass, 2012), 184, 185.

Closing Quote: Alan Autry, *http://www.brainyquote.com*, (Brainy Quote, BrainyMedia, Inc., 2017)

CHAPTER 10

Opening Quote: Martin Luther King Jr., *http://www.brainyquote.com*, (Brainy Quote, BrainyMedia, Inc., 2017)

Closing Quote: Stephen R. Covey, *The 8th Habit*, (Free Press, 2005)

APPENDIX
JIM'S FAVORITE LEADERSHIP RESOURCES

The 21 Irrefutable Laws of Leadership, John C. Maxwell

How to Win Friends and Influence People, Dale Carnegie

Monday Morning Leadership, David Cottrell

The Trust Edge, David Horsager

Leadership Axioms, Bill Hybels

25 Ways to Win with People, John C. Maxwell and Les Parrott, PH.D.

The Seven Habits of Highly Effective People, Steven R. Covey

Raising a Modern Day Knight, Robert Lewis

Spiritual Leadership, J. Oswald Sanders

Developing the Leader Within You, John C. Maxwell

Developing the Leaders Around You, John C. Maxwell

Never Fly Solo, Lt. Col. Rob "Waldo" Waldman

What Really Works, Paul Batz and Tim Schmidt

The Go-Giver, Bob Burg and John David Mann

Bring Jim into Your Business or Organization

Speaker – Author – Trainer – Coach

Jim knows the importance of choosing the correct speaker for your organization. His interactive and engaging style will bring your meeting to life as he customizes a message that's sure to have a positive impact on your audience.

CONTACT JIM TODAY TO
BEGIN THE CONVERSATION
JimZugschwert.com

CPSIA information can be obtained
at www.ICGtesting.com
Printed in the USA
BVHW07s1420030718
520751BV00001B/1/P